COLORFUL
KNITS

FOR YOU AND YOUR CHILD

COLORFUL KNITS

FOR YOU AND YOUR CHILD

OVER 25 ORIGINAL KNITWEAR DESIGNS

ZOË MELLOR

Trafalgar Square Publishing

*For my mother, Veronika, my father, Ray, and
for Eva, for all their support*

First published in the United States of
America in 1997 by Trafalgar Square
Publishing, North Pomfret, Vermont 05053

First published in Great Britain in 1997
by Collins & Brown Limited

Printed and bound in Spain by Graficromo

1 3 5 7 9 8 6 4 2

ISBN 1-57076-080-2

Library of Congress Catalog
Card Number: 96-61773

Editor : Margot Richardson
Designer: Jerry Goldie
Photography: Joey Toller
Hair and makeup: Hitoko Honbu at Hers
Styling: Zoë Mellor
Reproduction by Classic Scan

Contents

INTRODUCTION

Ever since I started my knitwear business people have been asking me for patterns of my work. Therefore I was very excited to be asked to write this book and to be able to share some of my favourite designs with you.

Having been brought up in the Caribbean with an architect as a father, my attention has always been drawn to form and colour and I find that it is the way that colours work together that inspire me and bring my work to life.

I enjoy painting and it is from playing with paints that I will often spring upon an idea for a sweater. My aim is to produce modern yet classical knitwear inspired by the old fashioned values of a time when children played with wooden toys.

I know people find the idea of colour knitting complicated but it really isn't. If you can knit with two colours then you can knit with ten. Remember, you are only knitting with one colour at a time. I have tried to mix simple designs with more intricate ones to cater for knitters of all abilities. All the charts are straightforward with easy-to-knit, simple shaping.

My business has been mainly focused on childrenswear and mothers would often say to me that there was never anything colourful for them to wear and that they felt left out. As you will see, many of the designs in this book are in both adult and children's sizes, as I believe colour should be for everyone !

Through these designs I hope to share their sense of fun and 'joie de vivre' with you. Happy knitting!

Zoë Mellor

Zoë Mellor

Harlequin jacket ⑨
(see page 38)

Elephant sweater
(see page 42)

Red bird sweater ⑪

(see page 44)

Folklore cardigan
(see page 46)

Dog sweater and bag (see page 49)

13

14   **Camel jacket**
(see page 51)

Farmyard sweater 15

(see page 53)

Pirate jacket (see page 56)

Circus jacket
(see page 58)

Coloured cables sweater and hat 21

(see page 61 and 62)

Kelim jacket (adult) and stripy moss-stitch sweater (child)
(see pages 63 and 65)

Stripy moss-stitch sweater
(see page 65)

Hearts sweater (left) and dolly mixture waistcoat **25**
(see pages 66 and 68)

Hearts sweater
(see page 66)

(see page 70)

Mexican sweater and jacket (child's)

(see page 70)

29

Stripy hat
(see page 74)

Ladybird sweater 33

(see page 75)

(see page 76)

36 **Tiger waistcoat**
(see page 77)

Stripes and spots sweater (right)
(see page 79)

HARLEQUIN JACKET

SIZES (CHILD)	1	2	3	4	5
to fit years	1-2	3-4	5-6	7-8	9-10
actual chest cm(ins)	66(26)	74(29)	81(32)	86(34)	89(35)
back length cm(ins) excluding edging	31(12)	38(15)	43(17)	46(18)	48(19)
sleeve seam cm(ins)	20(8)	28(11)	33(13)	36(14)	38(15)

SIZES (ADULT)	6	7	8
to fit size	S	M	L
actual bust cm(ins)	97(38)	107(42)	117(46)
back length cm(ins) excluding edging	53(21)	53(21)	53(21)
sleeve seam cm(ins)	43(17)	43(17)	43(17)

MATERIALS
Rowan Handknit Dk cotton 50g balls

SIZES	1	2	3	4	5	6	7	8
turkish plum 277	2	2	2	3	4	5	5	5
rosso 215	2	3	3	4	5	4	4	4
gooseberry 219	1	1	1	1	2	2	2	2
sunkissed 231	1	1	1	1	2	2	2	2
flame 254	1	1	1	1	2	2	2	2
summer pudding 243	1	1	1	1	2	2	2	2
powder 217	1	1	1	1	2	2	2	2
basil 221	1	1	1	1	2	2	2	2

1 pair each 3mm (US 2) and 4mm (US 5) needles, 5 buttons.

TENSION
20 sts by 28 rows = 10cm (4ins) square over stocking stitch using 4mm (US 5) needles.

ABBREVIATIONS
see page 80

BACK
Using 4mm (US 5) needles and rosso for child version, turkish plum for adult version cast on 69(75:81:85:89:95:105:115) sts. Working in stocking stitch, follow graph.

LEFT AND RIGHT FRONTS
Using 4mm (US 5) needles and rosso for child version and turkish plum for adult version cast on 34(37:40:42:44:47:52:57) sts. Working in stocking stitch, follow graph.

SLEEVES
Using 3mm (US 2) needles and turkish plum cast on 34(36:38:40:42:45:45:45) sts and work 8(8:10:10:10:9:9:9) rows in moss stitch.
Row 10: **Sizes 6:7:8** moss 7 *inc, moss 9* three times, inc, moss 7 *(49 sts)*.
Change to 4mm (US 5) needles and stocking stitch. Follow graph.
Sizes 7 and 8: repeat patt as on rows 75-83 over 95 sts. Cast off.

BUTTONBAND (Child version)
Using 3mm (US 2) needles and rosso cast on 6 sts and work in moss stitch until band, when slightly stretched, fits front to neck shaping. Cast off. Sew into place. Mark positions for 5 buttonholes, the first

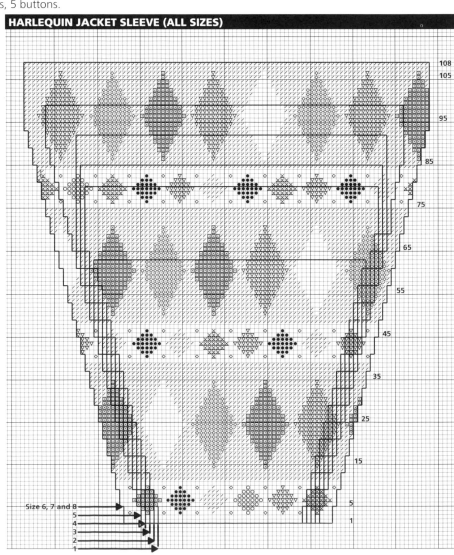

HARLEQUIN JACKET SLEEVE (ALL SIZES)

Size 6, 7 and 8

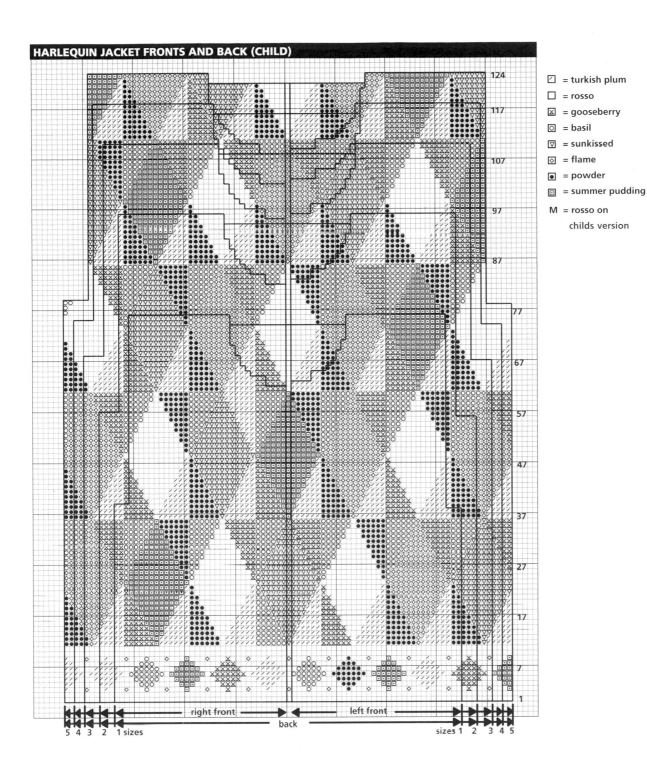

☑	= turkish plum
☐	= rosso
⊠	= gooseberry
⊡	= basil
▽	= sunkissed
⊙	= flame
●	= powder
⊡	= summer pudding
M	= rosso on childs version

BUTTONHOLE BAND (Child version)

and last 1cm(½in) from top and bottom edges, the remaining 3 evenly spaced between.

As buttonband but making buttonholes to match marked positions by: moss 2, k2tog, yrn, moss 2.

COLLAR (Child version)

Join shoulder seams. With RS facing and using 3mm (US 2) needles and rosso pick up and knit 73(77:79:83:85) sts around neck, beginning and ending at centre of front bands. Work as follows:
Rows 1-2: k2, moss to last 2 sts, k2
Row 3: k2, moss to last 3 sts, inc, k2
Repeat row 3 until collar measures 6cm (2½ins). Cast off loosely in moss stitch.

BUTTONBAND (Adult version)

Using 3mm (US 2) needles and turkish plum cast on 7 sts. Work 4 rows in moss stitch.
Make buttonhole: moss 2, k2tog, yrn, moss 3.
Make 4 more buttonholes at 8cm (3ins) intervals. Continue with band until when slightly stretched it fits around garment neck and front opening.

POINTED EDGING

Using 4mm (US 5) needles and M cast on 2 sts. Work as follows:
Row 1: k2
Row 2: inc, k1
Row 3: k1 p1, inc
Row 4: inc, k1 p1 k1
Row 5-8: moss stitch, inc at shaped edge on every row: *9 sts*

Row 9: moss stitch
Row 10-16: dec at shaped edge on each row, moss stitch   *2 sts*
Repeat rows 1-16 until straight edge fits lower edge of garment excluding front bands, ending after a complete repeat.

MAKING UP

Child version: Join side seams. Set in sleeves, markers to side seam (see diagram on page 80). Join sleeve seams. Attach edging to bottom of garment, omitting front bands. Sew on buttons. Weave in any loose ends.
Adult version: Join shoulder seams. Attach front band, then follow as for child version.

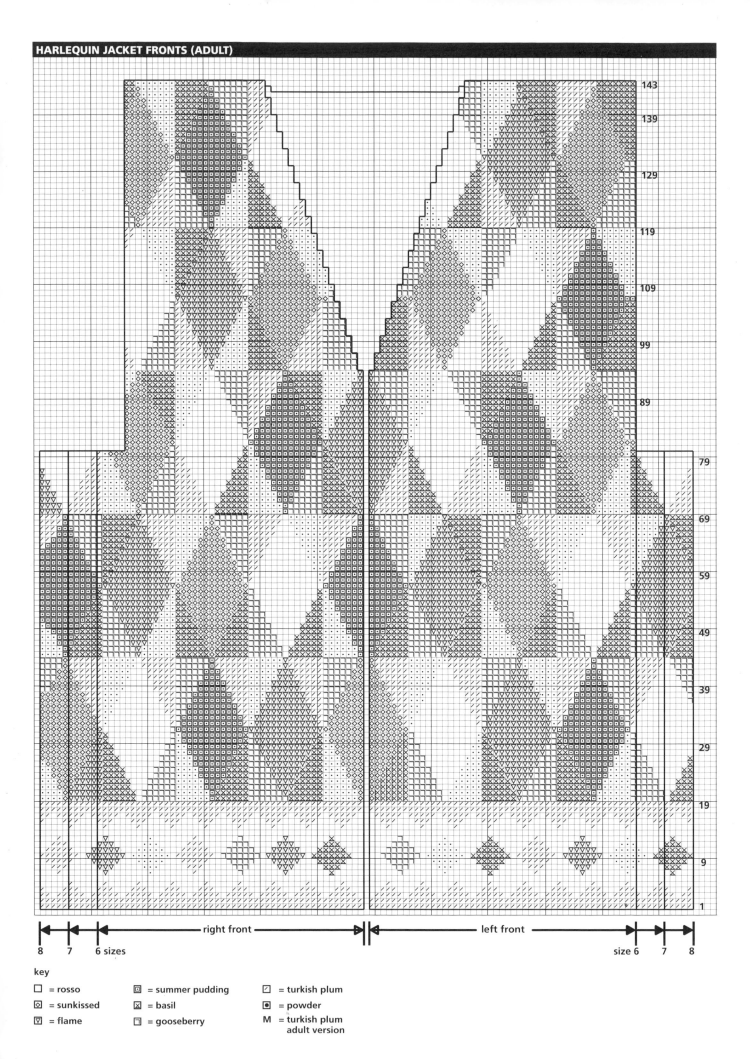

key

□ = rosso	▣ = summer pudding	⬚ = turkish plum		
⊡ = sunkissed	⊠ = basil	⬓ = powder		
▽ = flame	⬛ = gooseberry	M = turkish plum adult version		

40 **Harlequin jacket**

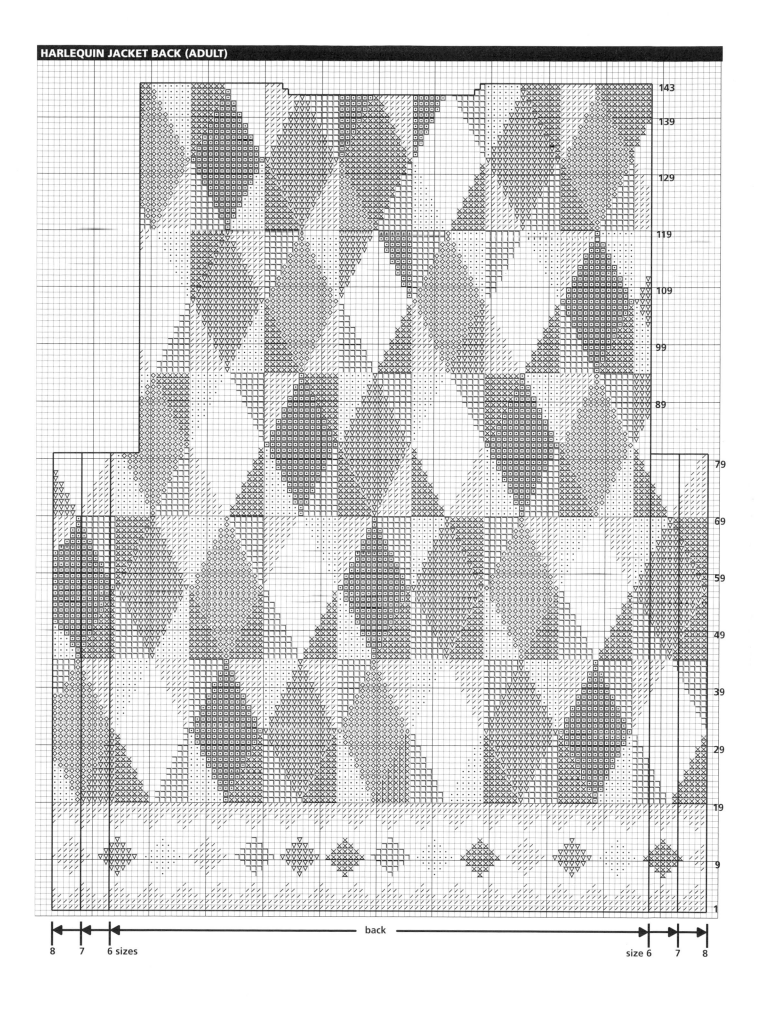

back

8   7   6 sizes   size 6   7   8

Harlequin jacket ●41

ELEPHANT SWEATER

SIZES	1	2	3
to fit years	1-2	3-4	5-6
actual chest cm(ins)	69(27)	76(30)	82(32¼)
back length cm(ins)	36(14¼)	41(16¼)	47(18½)
sleeve seam cm(ins)	22(8½)	28(11)	31(12)

MATERIALS
Rowan Handknit Dk cotton 50g balls

M = turkish plum 277	6	7	8
basil 221	1	1	1
flame 254	1	1	1
powder 217	1	1	1
sunkissed 231	1	1	1
rosso 215	2	2	2

1 pair each 3¼mm (US 3) and 4mm (US 5) needles, stitch holders.

TENSION
20 sts by 28 rows = 10cm (4ins) square over stocking stitch using 4mm (US 5) needles.

ABBREVIATIONS
see page 80

BACK
Using 3¼mm (US 3) needles and rosso cast on 68(76:84) sts. Change to M and work 8 rows rib as follows:
Every row: *k2 p2*; rep to end.
Change to 4mm (US 5) needles and stocking stitch and work 15 rows from border chart. Change to main chart starting at row 11(7:1) with a **purl** row. Foll chart omitting elephant and place 3 diamond or star motifs (as on background of sweater) in space where elephant was. Place these randomly at your discretion.
Size 2 only: Rows 7, 8 and 9 on the main chart (ie the first 3 rows) omit part of star motifs.

FRONT
Work rib as back, then work border chart. Now work in stocking stitch from front chart with elephant. Beg chart row 11(7:1) with a **purl** row.

SLEEVES
Using 3¼mm (US 3) needles and rosso ,cast on 36(38:40) sts. Change to M and work 8 rows in k2 p2 rib as for back for 1st and 3rd sizes.
Size 2 only:
Row 1: k2 *p2 k2* to end
Row 2: p2 *k2 p2* to end.
Repeat rows 1-2 three times.
All sizes: Change to 4mm (US 5) needles and stocking stitch. Follow graph to end and cast off.

NECKBAND
Join right shoulder seam. With RS facing, using 3¼mm (US 3) needles and M, pick up and k 18(20:21) sts from left front neck, 8(8:10) sts from centre neck, 18(20:21) sts from right front neck, 2 sts from side back

neck, 20(22:24) sts from centre back, and 2 sts from side back neck: *68(74,80) sts.* Work 5 rows in k2 p2 rib as for front. Change to rosso and cast off loosely using a 4mm (US 5) needle.

MAKING UP
Join shoulder and neckband seams. Join side seams. Set in sleeve head, marker to side seam (see diagram on page 80) and stitch into place. Join sleeve seam. Weave in any loose ends.

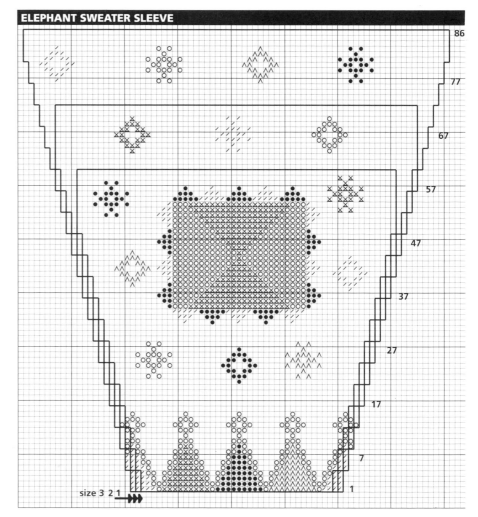

ELEPHANT SWEATER SLEEVE

size 3 2 1

□ = turkish plum (M)   ◩ = flame   ◙ = sunkissed
◪ = basil   ◉ = powder   ⊠ = rosso

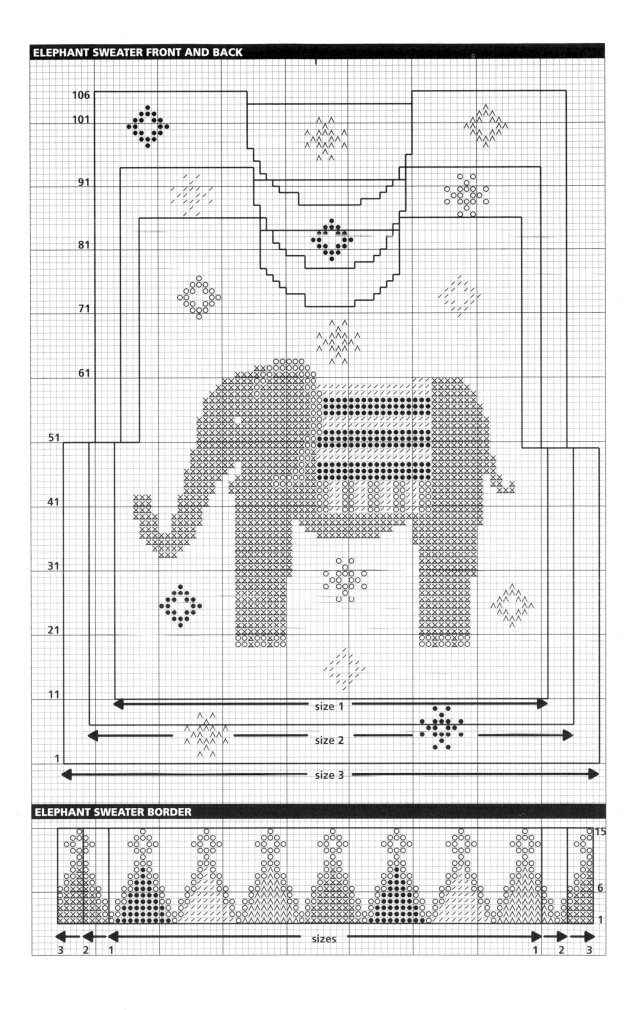

size 1

size 2

size 3

ELEPHANT SWEATER BORDER

sizes

RED BIRD SWEATER

SIZES	1	2	3
to fit years	1-2	3-4	5-6
actual chest cm(ins)	65(25½)	76(30)	81(32)
back length cm(ins)	33(13)	38(15)	46(18)
sleeve seam cm(ins)	22(8½)	28(11)	31(12)

MATERIALS

Rowan Handknit Dk cotton 50g balls

M = rosso 215	7	8	9
bleached 263	1	2	2
flame 254	1	1	1
powder 217	1	1	1
popcorn 229	1	1	1
basil 221	1	1	1
turkish plum 277	1	1	1

1 pair each 3¼mm (US 3) and 4mm (US 5) needles, stitch holders.

TENSION

20 sts by 28 rows = 10cm (4ins) square over stocking stitch using 4mm (US 5) needles.

ABBREVIATIONS

see page 80

BACK AND FRONT

Using 3¼mm (US 3) needles and rosso cast on 64(76:82) sts and work as follows:
Row 1: p2(0:3) *k2 p2* to last 2(0:3) sts, k2(0:3)
Row 2: add powder and keeping floats to WS of work: WS facing, p2(0:3) powder, *k2 rosso p2 powder* to last 2(0:3) sts, k2(0:3) rosso
Row 3: p2(0:3) rosso *k2 powder p2 rosso* to last 2(0:3) sts, k2(0:3) powder
Rows 4-9: repeat rows 2-3 three times.
Row 10: using rosso p2(0:3) *k2 p2* to last 2(0:3) sts, k2(0:3)
Change to 4mm (US 5) needles and stocking stitch. Follow graph, placing centre neck sts on holders.

SLEEVES

Using 3¼mm (US 3) needles and rosso cast on 36(38:40) sts and work as follows:
Row 1: p2(3:2) *k2 p2* to last 2(3:2) sts, k2(3:2)
Row 2: add powder and keeping floats to WS of work: WS facing, p2(3:2) powder *k2 rosso p2 powder* to last 2(3:2) sts, k2(3:2) rosso
Row 3: p2(3:2) rosso *k2 powder p2 rosso* to last 2(3:2) sts, k2(3:2) powder
Rows 4-7: repeat rows 2-3 twice
Row 8: Using rosso p2(3:2) *k2 p2* to last 2(3:2) sts, k2(3:2)
Change to 4mm (US 5) needles and stocking stitch. Follow graph.

NECKBAND

Join right shoulder seam.
Using 3¼mm (US 3) needles and rosso, with RS facing, pick up and knit 14(14:16) sts from side front neck, 14 sts from holder, 14(14:16) sts from side front neck, 3sts

RED BIRD SWEATER FRONT AND BACK (SIZE 1)

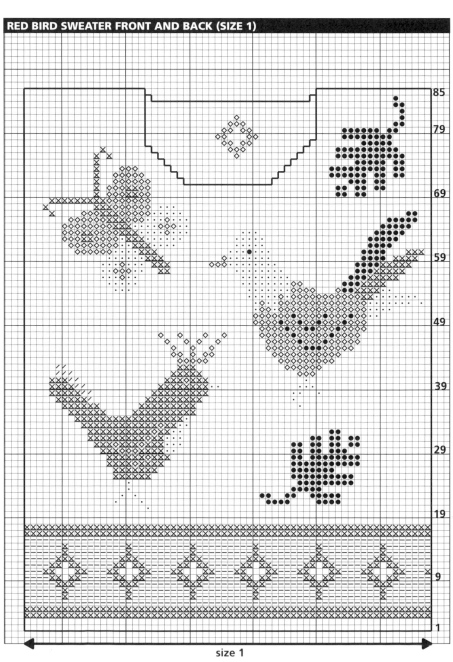

size 1

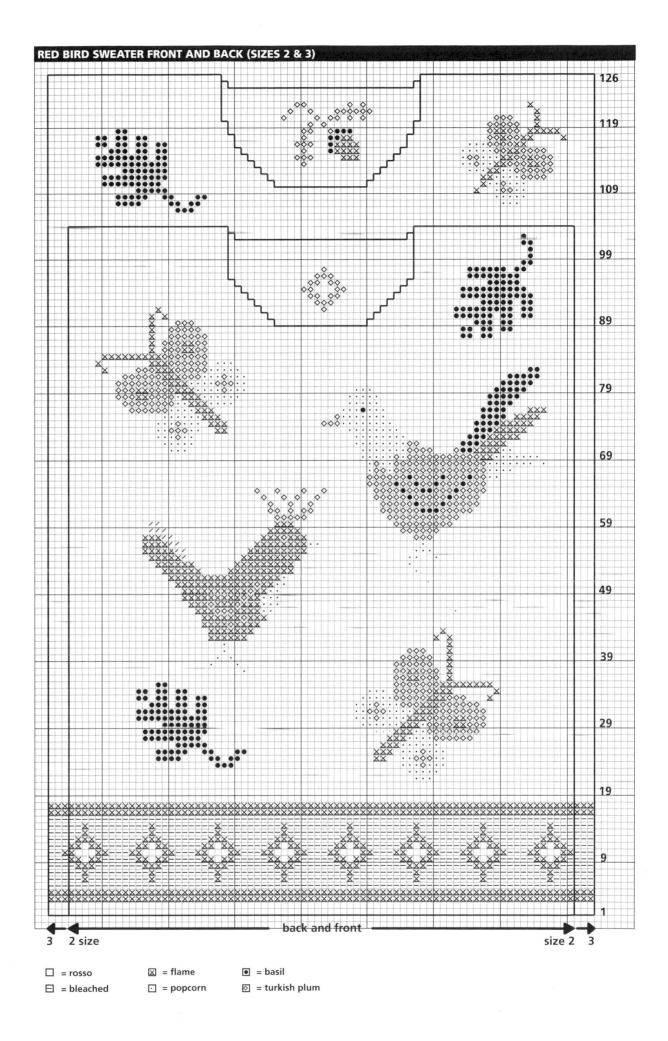

back and front

3   2 size   size 2   3

☐ = rosso   ⊠ = flame   ◉ = basil
⊟ = bleached   ⊡ = popcorn   ◇ = turkish plum

Red bird sweater   **45**

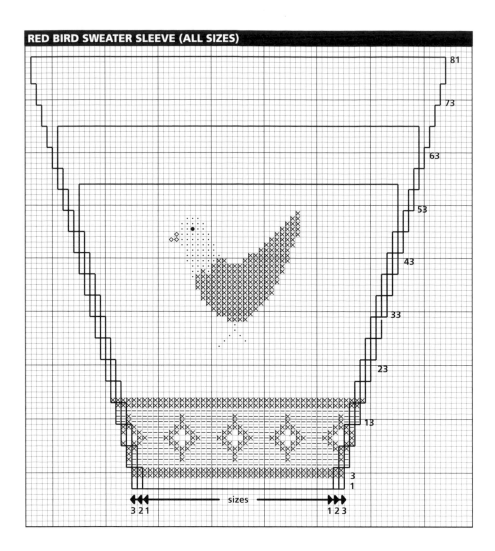

RED BIRD SWEATER SLEEVE (ALL SIZES)

81
73
63
53
43
33
23
13
3
1

sizes
3 2 1   1 2 3

from side back neck, 24(26:28) sts from holder and 3 sts from side back neck. Work 5(6:6) rows in two-coloured rib as on welts and cuffs. Cast off loosely using powder.

MAKING UP
Join left shoulder seam and neckband. Set in sleeve head, stitch into place. Join sleeve and side seams. Weave in any loose ends.

FOLKLORE CARDIGAN

SIZES

to fit	S	M	L
actual bust cm(ins)	102(40)	110(43)	117(46)
back length cm(ins)	51(20)	51(20)	51(20) (excluding edging)
sleeve seam cm(ins)	46(18)	46(18)	46(18)

MATERIALS
Rowan Designer Double Knitting wool 50g balls

M = ecru 649	15	16	17
blue 696	1	1	1
red 634	1	1	1
light green 635	1	1	1
dark green 685	1	1	1
orange 699	2	2	2
pink 070	2	2	2
fern 364 (chenille)	1	1	1

1 pair each 3¼mm (US 3) and 3¾mm (US 4) needles, 5 buttons.

TENSION
24 sts by 32 rows = 10cm (4ins) square over stocking stitch using 3¾mm (US 4) needles.

ABBREVIATIONS
see page 80

BACK
Using 3¾mm (US 4) needles and orange, cast on 120(130:140) sts. Working in

stocking stitch, follow graph.

RIGHT AND LEFT FRONTS
Using 3¾mm (US 4) needles and orange, cast on 60(65:70) sts. Working in stocking stitch, follow graph.

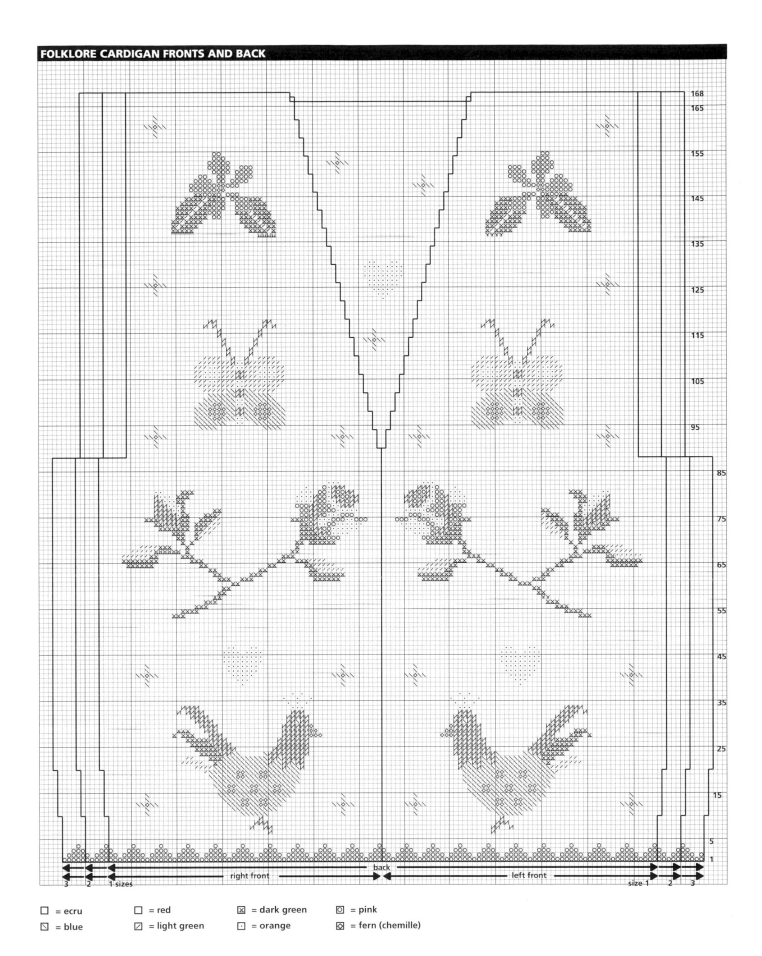

☐ = ecru	☐ = red
◩ = blue	◪ = light green
⊠ = dark green	⊡ = orange
▣ = pink	⊠ = fern (chemille)

SLEEVES

Using 3¼mm (US 3) needles and pink, cast on 55 sts. Change to M and work 15 rows in moss stitch.
Row 16: *moss 5, inc, moss 5* five times

60 sts

Change to 3¾mm (US 4) needles and stocking stitch. Follow graph.

FRONT BAND

Join shoulder and side seams. Using 3¼mm (US 3) needles and M cast on 9 sts. Work 4

rows in moss stitch.
Row 5: Make buttonhole: moss 3, cast off 2 sts, moss 4
Row 6: moss 4, cast on 2 sts, moss 3
Continue in moss stitch, making 4 further buttonholes at 8cm (3ins) intervals, then

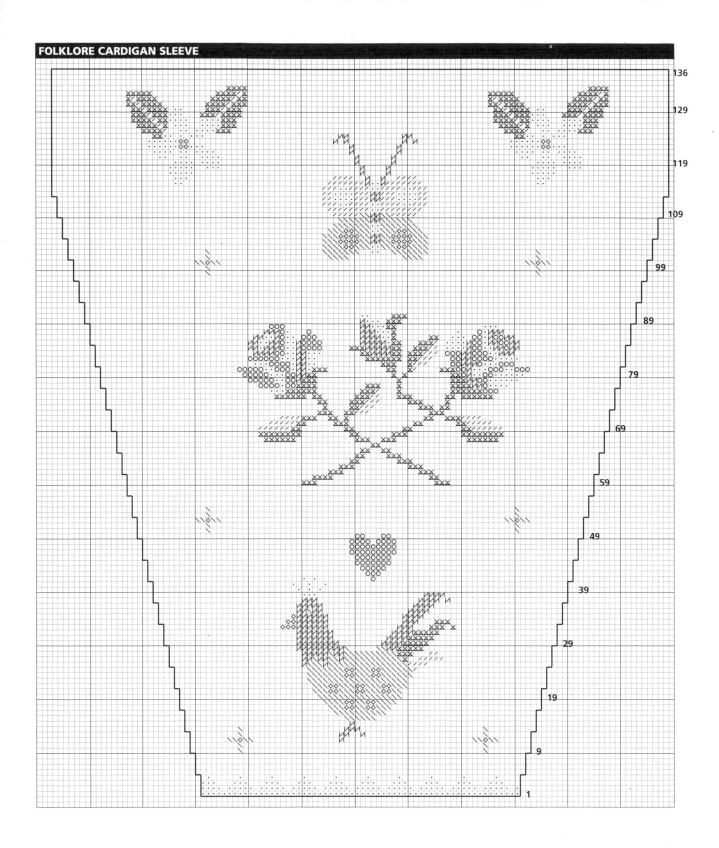

136
129
119
109
99
89
79
69
59
49
39
29
19
9
1

continue until band fits around front edge.
Attach front band.

POINTED EDGING

Using 3¾mm (US 4) needles and pink, cast
on 2sts.
Row 1: k2
Row 2: inc, k1
Row 3: k1 p1 inc
Row 4: inc, k1 p1 k1
Rows 5-8: moss stitch, inc at shaped edge
on every row   *9 sts*
Row 9: moss stitch

Rows 10-16: dec at shaped edge on each
row, moss stitch   *2 sts*
Repeat rows 1-16 until straight edge fits
lower edge of garment excluding front
bands, ending after a complete pattern
repeat.

MAKING UP

Set in sleeve head, markers to side seam
(see diagram on page 80). Stitch into
place. Join sleeve seams. Weave in any
loose ends. Sew on buttons.

DOG BAG

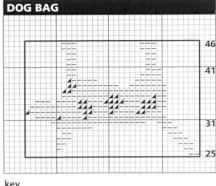

Bag Size: 23cm x 18cm x 5cm
(9ins x 7ins x 2ins)

MATERIALS
Rowan Designer Double Knitting wool

	50g balls
Main = blue 696	3 balls
Small amounts of black 062 and white 649	

1 pair each 3mm (US 2) and 3¾mm (US 4) needles, 2 buttons.

TENSION
24 sts by 32 rows = 10cm (4ins) square over stocking stitch using 3¾mm (US 4) needles.

ABBREVIATIONS
see page 80

METHOD
Begin at top front edge. Using 3¾mm (US 4) needles and M cast on 55 sts and knit 4 rows. Change to stocking stitch. Work 24 rows.
Row 25: Start dog: k11 M, k2 white, k42M (work dog upside down)
Rows 26-46: Complete dog from graph. Cont in stocking stitch until work measures 18cm (7ins). Change to moss stitch. Cont until work measures 23cm (9ins).
Cast on 11 sts beg next 2 rows. Cont in moss stitch until work measures 41cm (16ins). Cast off 11 sts beg next 2 rows.
Cont until work measures 48cm (19ins).
Make buttonholes: moss 5, cast off 2 sts,

moss 41, cast off 2 sts, moss 5.
Next row: moss 5, cast on 2 sts, moss 41, cast on 2 sts, moss 5.
Work 6 more rows. Cast off in moss stitch.

STRAP
Using 3mm (US 2) needles cast on 11 sts and work 75cm (29½ins) in moss stitch. Cast off.
NOTE: Strap length can be altered to fit size of child.

MAKING UP
Join BF to FC
Join AC to BD
Sew on buttons, weave in loose ends.
Attach strap ends to DH

HOW TO LINE BAG
Taking fabric of your choice cut out bag shape, adding a 1cm(½in) seam allowance all round. Do this by laying down the flat bag shape and drawing around it on to the fabric. Do the same with the knitted shoulder strap making the lining at least 5cm (2ins) longer as the knitted strap will increase in length when being fed through the sewing machine. Bag out the lining and knitted bag by sewing up the side seams. Attach the lining by sewing neatly around the top of the bag, pinning it in place as you sew. Both seams should be concealed on the inside of the lining. Add 2 buttons to the front of the bag corresponding to the buttonholes knitted on the flap.

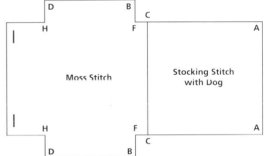

DOG BAG

key
☐ = blue   ⊡ = white   ☑ = black

DOG SWEATER

SIZES	1	2	3	4
to fit years	1-2	3-4	5-6	7-8
actual chest cm(ins)	66(26)	77(30½)	84(33)	89(35)
back length cm(ins)	33(13)	38(15)	46(18)	51(20)
sleeve seam cm(ins)	22(8½)	28(11)	30(12)	33(13)

MATERIALS
Rowan Designer Double Knitting wool 50g balls

M = red 632	6	7	8	9
white 649	1	1	1	1
yellow 610	1	1	1	1
black 062	1	1	1	1
navy 607	1	1	1	1

1 pair each 3¼mm (US 3) and 3¾mm (US 4) needles, stitch holders

TENSION
24 sts by 32 rows = 10cm (4ins) square over stocking stitch using 3¾mm (US 4) needles.

ABBREVIATIONS
see page 80

FRONT

Using 3¼mm (US 3) needles and navy cast on 86(92:98:104) sts. Change to M and work 12 rows in moss stitch.Change to 3¾mm (US 4) needles and stocking stitch. Follow graph, placing centre neck stitches on holder. **Note**: dog motif correctly placed on graph for sizes 1(2), for sizes 3(4) place motif 24(40) rows higher, omitting daisies in that area and placing 2 daisies in vacated dog area.

BACK

As for front, but place 2 more daisies instead of dog motif.

SLEEVES

Using 3¼mm (US 3) needles and navy cast on 39(41:43:45) sts. Change to M and work 12 rows in moss stitch. Change to 3¾mm (US 4) needles and stocking stitch, follow graph.

NECKBAND

Join right shoulder seam. With RS facing and using 3¼mm (US 3) needles and M, pick up and knit 16(16:18:20) sts from side front neck, 14(16:16:18) sts from holder, 16(16:18:20) sts from side front neck, 2 sts from side back neck, 26(28:30:32) sts from holder, 2 sts from side back neck. Work 5 rows in moss stitch. Cast off loosely using navy.

MAKING UP

Join left shoulder seam and neckband. Join side seams. Set in sleeve head, placing markers at side seams (see diagram on page 80). Join sleeve seam. Weave in any loose ends.

key
☐ = red
☐ = white
☒ = yellow
◢ = black

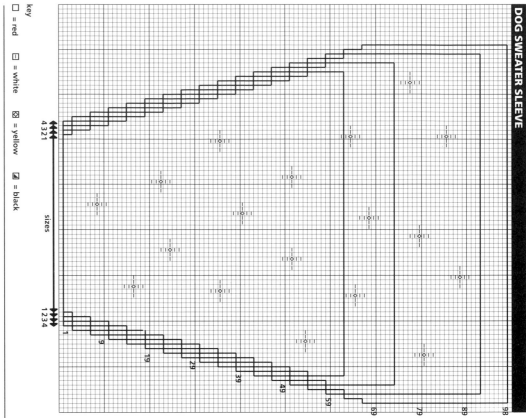

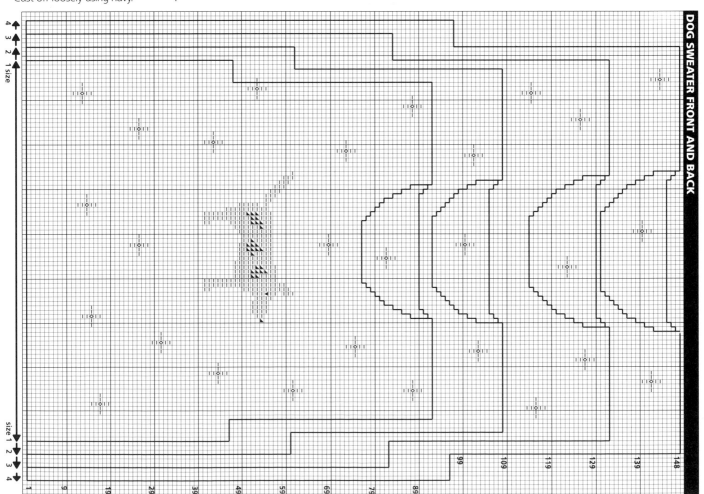

CAMEL JACKET

SIZES	1	2	3
to fit loosely years	1-2	3-4	5-6
actual chest cm(ins)	66(26)	76(30)	84(33)
back length cm(ins)	30(12)	36(14)	44(17) (excluding edging)
sleeve seam cm(ins)	22(8½)	28(11)	31(12)

MATERIALS

Rowan Designer Double Knitting wool 50g balls

	1	2	3
M = blue 629	7	7	8
A = light green 404	1	1	1
B = dark green 685	1	1	1
C = navy 607	2	2	2
D = orange 699	1	1	1
E = pink 630	1	1	1
G = gold 610	1	1	1
H = red 634	1	1	2

1 pair each 3¼mm (US 3) and 3¾mm (US 4) needles, 5 buttons.

TENSION

24 sts by 32 rows = 10cm (4ins) square over stocking stitch using 3¾mm (US 4) needles.

ABBREVIATIONS

see page 80

BACK

Using 3¾mm (US 4) needles and C cast on 79(89:99) sts and work in stocking stitch from graph.
Size 1: rows 1-20, 31-76 and 101-110

Size 2: rows 1-82 and 10 -110
Size 3: rows 1-110
Work 20(20:26) more rows in coloured stripes.
Shape neck: patt 24(26:30) sts, cast off 23(25:27) sts, patt to end.
On 24(26:30) sts:
*Row 1: patt
Rows 2-3: dec neck edge, patt
Row 4: cast off*
Rejoin yarn to remaining sts at neck edge.
Work * to *.

LEFT FRONT

Using 3¾mm (US 4) needles and C cast on 39(44:49) sts and work in stocking stitch from graph.
Size 1: rows 1-20, 31-76 and 101-110
Size 2: rows 1-82 and 101-110
Size 3: rows 1-110
Work 5(5:9) more rows in coloured stripes.
** **Shape neck:**
Row 1: Cast off 6(7:7) sts, patt to end
Rows 2-5: dec neck edge, patt
Row 6: patt
Row 7: dec neck edge, patt

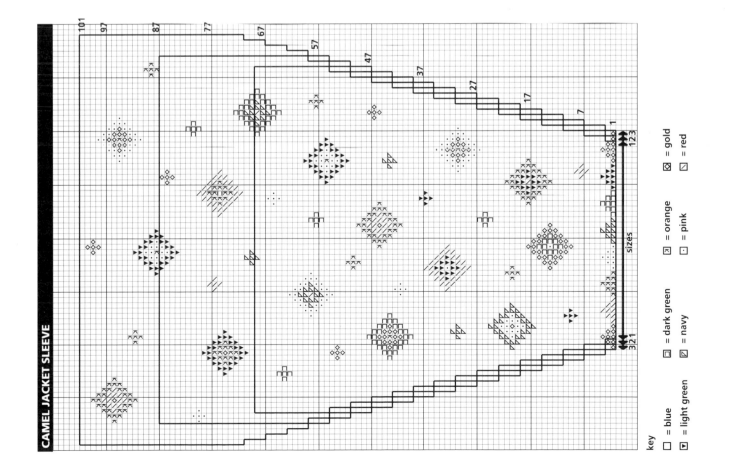

key
☐ = blue
▶ = light green
⊡ = dark green
⊠ = navy
⊗ = gold
☑ = red
⊠ = orange
⊡ = pink

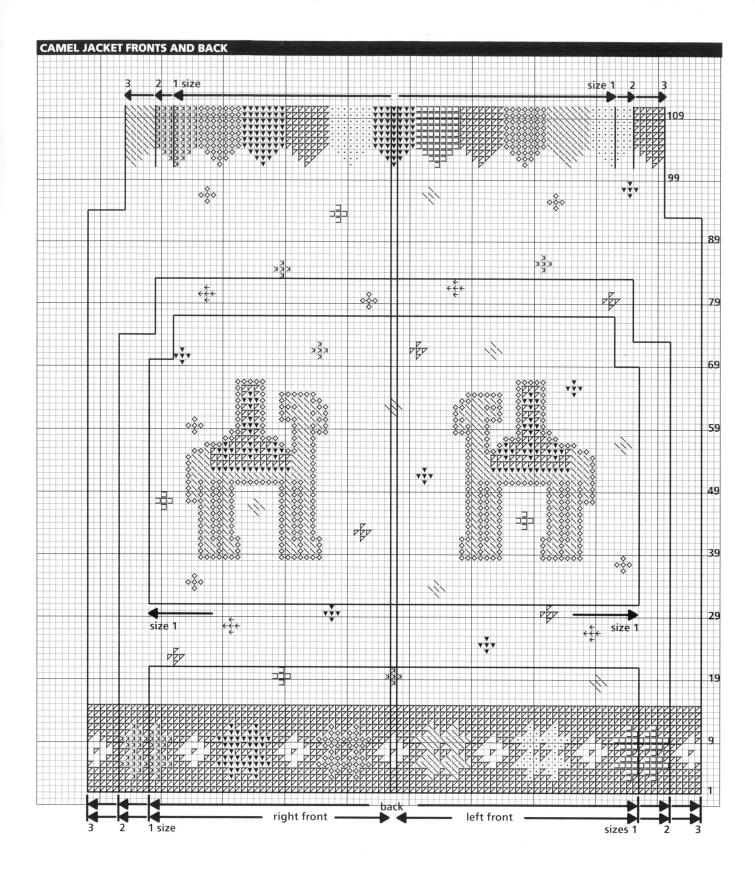

Rows 8-11: as rows 6-7**
Sizes 1 and 2: Work 6 more rows. Cast off.
Size 3: Rows 12-13: as rows 6-7.
Work 6 more rows. Cast off.

RIGHT FRONT
As left front to row 110.
Work 6(6:10) more rows in coloured stripes
Work ** to ** of neck shaping.
Sizes 1 and 2: Work 5 more rows. Cast off.

Size 3: Rows 12-13: as rows 6-7
Work 5 more rows. Cast off.

SLEEVES
Using 3¼mm (US 3) needles and M cast on 37(39:41) sts and work 6 rows in moss stitch.
Change to 3¾mm (US 4) needles and stocking stitch. Follow graph.

BUTTONBAND
Using 3¼mm (US 3) needles and M cast on

7 sts and work in moss stitch until band when slightly stretched fits front edge. Sew into place.

BUTTONHOLE BAND
Make buttonhole band as buttonband, but make 5 buttonholes evenly spaced along band the first and last 1cm (½in) from top and bottom edges. Sew into place.
Make buttonholes:
Row 1: moss 2, cast off 2 sts, moss 3.
Row 2: moss 3, cast on 2 sts, moss 2.

POINTED EDGING

Using 3¼mm (US 3) needles and M cast on 2 sts.
Row 1: k2
Row 2: inc, k1
Row 3: k1, p1, inc
Row 4: inc, k1 p1 k1
Rows 5-8: moss stitch, inc at shaped edge on every row   **9 sts**
Row 9: moss stitch
Rows 10-16: dec at shaped edge on each row, moss stitch   **2 sts**.
Repeat rows 1-16 until straight edge fits lower edge of garment, excluding front bands, ending after a complete patt repeat.

COLLAR

Join shoulder seams. With RS facing and using 3¼mm (US 3) needles and M, pick up and knit 77(81:87) sts around neck, starting and finishing halfway across front bands. Work as follows:
Rows 1-2: k2, moss to last 2 sts, k2
Row 3: k2, moss to last 3 sts, inc, k2.
Repeat row 3 until collar measures 6cm (2½ins). Cast off loosely in moss stitch.

MAKING UP

Join side seams. Set in sleeve head markers to side seam, (see diagram on page 80). Stitch into place. Join sleeve seams. Weave in any loose ends. Sew on buttons.

FARMYARD SWEATER

SIZES	1	2	3	6	7
to fit	1-2yrs	3-4yrs	5-6yrs	S-M	M-L
actual chest/bust cm(ins)	66(26)	80(31½)	84(33)	107(42)	117(46)
back length cm(ins)	31(12)	36(14)	45(18)	63(25)	63(25)
sleeve seam cm(ins)	19(7½)	25(10)	30(12)	46(18)	46(18)

(size 6 & 7 are adult sizes)

NOTE: back length does not include edging measurements.

MATERIALS

Rowan Handknit Dk cotton 50g balls

M = powder 217	6	8	10	17	19
bleached 263	1	1	1	3	3
rosso 215	1	1	1	2	2
popcorn 229	1	1	1	2	2
basil 221	1	1	1	2	2
turkish plum 277	1	1	1	2	2
port 245	1	1	1	2	2
raspberry 240	1	1	1	1	1
flame 245	1	1	1	2	2
black 252	1	1	1	1	1
fern 364 (chenille)	1	1	1	1	1

NOTE: colours above refer to child's light blue colourway. To make navy version M = turkish plum, and replace turkish plum with powder .

1 pair each 3¼mm (US 3) and 4mm (US 5) needles, stitch holders.

TENSION

20 sts by 28 rows = 10cm (4ins) square over stocking stitch using 4mm (US 5) needles.

ABBREVIATIONS

see page 80

BACK AND FRONT

Using 4mm (US 5) needles and M cast on 65(80:85:105:115) sts and follow graph. Work in stocking stitch and place centre neck sts on holders.

SLEEVES

Using 3¼mm (US 3) needles and turkish plum (use basil for adult colourway) cast on 35(37:39:45:45) sts and work 6(6:8:10:10)rows in moss stitch. Change to 4mm (US 5) needles and stocking stitch.

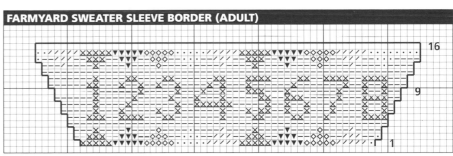

FARMYARD SWEATER SLEEVE BORDER (ADULT)

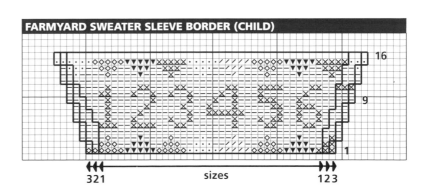

FARMYARD SWEATER SLEEVE BORDER (CHILD)

321   sizes   123

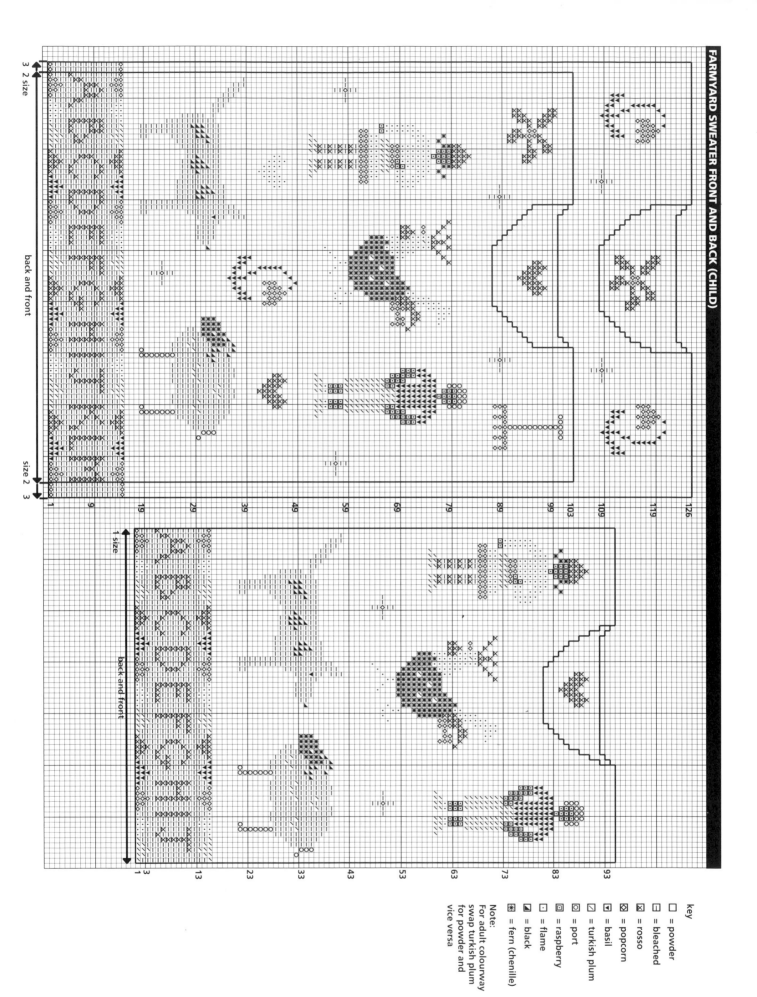

key

□ = powder
□ = bleached
⊠ = rosso
⊗ = popcorn
◄ = basil
╱ = turkish plum
○ = port
□ = raspberry
· = flame
◣ = black
⊞ = fern (chenille)

Note:
For adult colourway
swap turkish plum
for powder and
vice versa

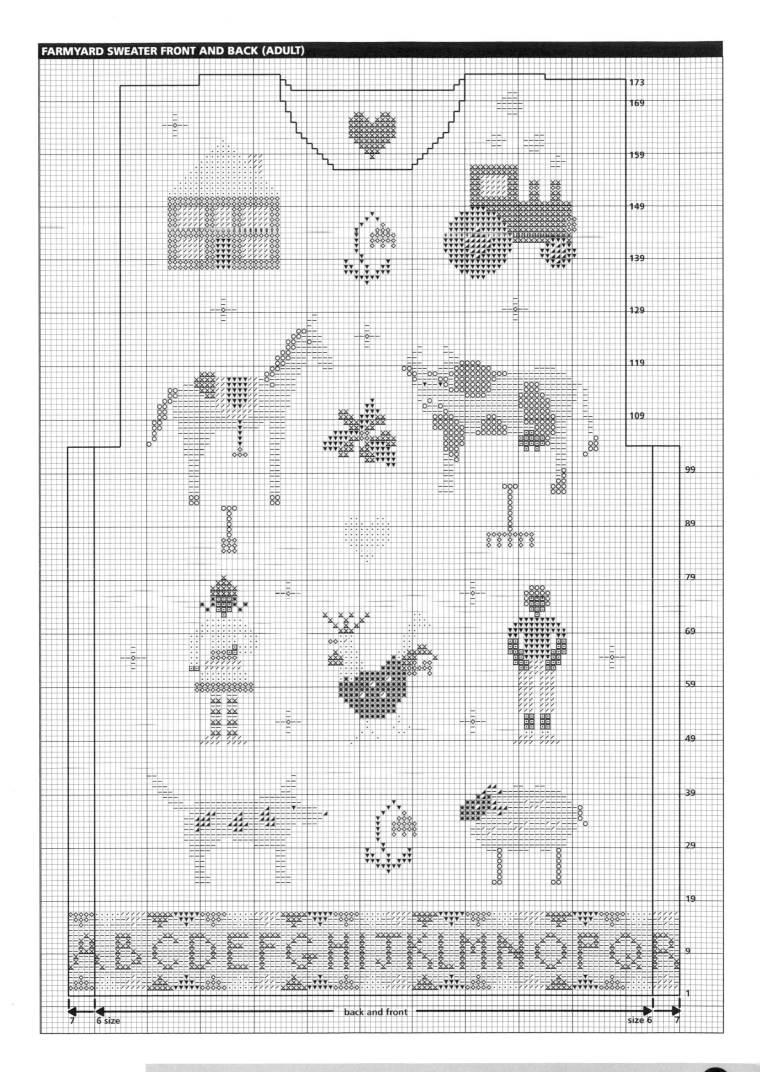

Work 16 rows from graph. Keeping inc every 4th row, cont as follows:
using M, moss stitch 5 rows; using contrast, stocking stitch 2(2:2:3:3) rows: using M, stocking stitch 1 row.
* to * forms patt repeat. The contrast is repeat 1 = flame; 2 = powder or turkish plum; 3 = rosso; 4 =popcorn; 5 =basil; 6-10 as 1-5, etc.
Continue in patt to 55(63:71:95:95) sts. Continue without shaping until work measures 19(25:30:46:46)cm or 7½ (10:12:18:18)ins. Place markers at each end of last row. Work further 4(5:5:6:6) rows. Cast off.

NECKBAND
Join right shoulder seam. With RS facing and using 3¼mm (US 3) needles and M pick up and knit 14(16:18:20:20) sts from side front neck 11(12:13:15:15) sts from holder, 14(16:18:20:20) sts from side front neck, 2(2:2:3:3) sts from side back neck, 23(24:25:31:31) sts from holder and 2(2:2:3:3) sts from side back neck. Work 5(5:6:8:8) rows in k2 p2 rib. Cast off in rib using basil for turkish plum version and turkish plum for powder version.

POINTED EDGING
Using 4mm (US 5) needles and M,cast on 2 sts.
Row 1: k2
Row 2: inc, k1

Row 3: k1 p1 inc
Row 4: inc, k1 p1 k1
Rows 5-8: moss stitch, inc at shaped edge on every row   **9 sts**
Row 9: moss stitch
Rows10-16: dec at shaped edge on each row, moss stitch.   **2 sts**
Repeat rows 1-16 until straight edge fits lower edge of garment, ending after a complete patt repeat.

MAKING UP
Join left shoulder seam and neckband. Join side seams. Set in sleeve head, markers to side seam: see diagram on page 80. Stitch into position. Join sleeve seams. Weave in any loose ends.

PIRATE JACKET

Sizes	1	2	3
to fit years	1-2	3-4	5-6
actual chest cm(ins)	65(25½)	76(30)	81(32)
sleeve length cm (ins)	22(8½)	25(10)	32(12½)
back length cm(ins)	33(13)	38(15)	46(18)

MATERIALS
Rowan Handknit Dk cotton 50g balls			
M = powder 217	6	7	8
turkish plum 277	1	2	2
rosso 215	1	1	1
bleached 263	1	1	1
sunkissed 231	1	1	1
flame 254	1	1	1
gooseberry 219	1	1	1
basil 221	1	1	1
black 252	1	1	1
raspberry 240	1	1	1
port 245	1	1	1

1 pair each 3¼ mm (US 3) and 4 mm (US 5) needles, 5 buttons.

TENSION
20 sts by 28 rows = 10cm (4ins) square over stocking stitch using 4mm (US 5) needles.

ABBREVIATIONS
see page 80

BACK
Using 3¼mm (US 3) needles and turkish plum cast on 65(76:82) sts and work 6(8:8) rows in moss stitch. Change to 4mm (US 5) needles and stocking stitch. Follow graph.
Size 1 only: Start pirate ship 4 rows lower than on graph and start neck shaping on row 87 of graph, casting off on row 89.
Size 2 only: Omit pirate banner motif by shoulders.

FRONTS
Using 3¼mm (US 3) needles and turkish plum cast on 32(38:41) sts and work 6(8:8) rows in moss stitch. Change to 4mm (US 5) needles and stocking stitch. Follow graph.

SLEEVES
Using 3¼mm (US 3) needles and turkish plum cast on 36(38:40) sts and work 6(8:8) rows in moss stitch. Change to 4mm (US 5) needles and stocking stitch. Follow graph.

BUTTONBAND
Using 3¼mm (US 3) needles and turkish plum cast on 6 sts and work in moss stitch until band, when slightly stretched, fits front to neck shaping. Cast off. Sew into place. Mark positions for 5 buttonholes, the first and last 1cm (½in) from top and bottom edges and remaining 3 evenly spaced between.

BUTTONHOLE BAND
Work to match buttonband making buttonholes to match button positions by: moss 2, k2tog, yrn, moss 2.

COLLAR
Join shoulder seams. Using 3¼mm (US 3) needles and turkish plum, with right side facing and beginning and ending at centre of front bands, pick up and knit 73(77:79) sts from neck. Work as follows:
Rows 1-2: k2, moss to last 2 sts, k2
Row 3: k2, moss to last 3 sts, inc, k2
Repeat row 3 until collar measures 6cm (2¾ins.). Cast off loosely in moss stitch.

MAKING UP
Join side seams. Set in sleeves, placing markers to side seam – see diagram on page 80 – and stitch into place. Join sleeve seams. Sew on buttons. Weave in any loose ends

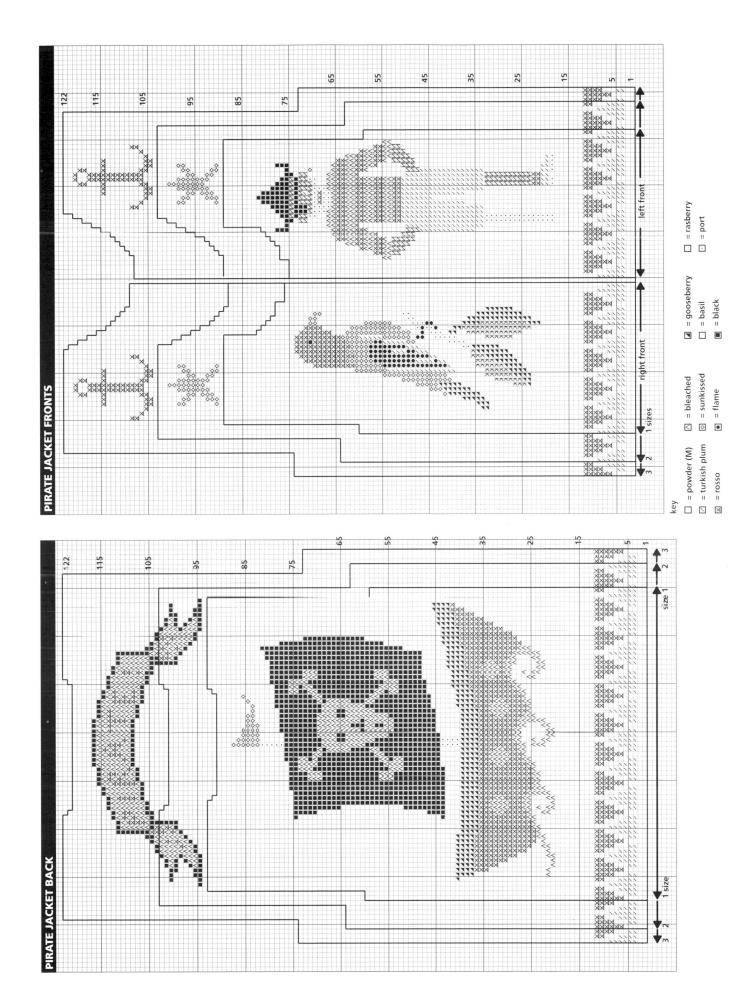

PIRATE JACKET FRONTS

PIRATE JACKET BACK

key

□ = powder (M)	⊠ = bleached	□ = gooseberry	□ = rasberry	
⊡ = turkish plum	⊙ = sunkissed	□ = basil	⊡ = port	
⊠ = rosso	⊡ = flame	▣ = black		

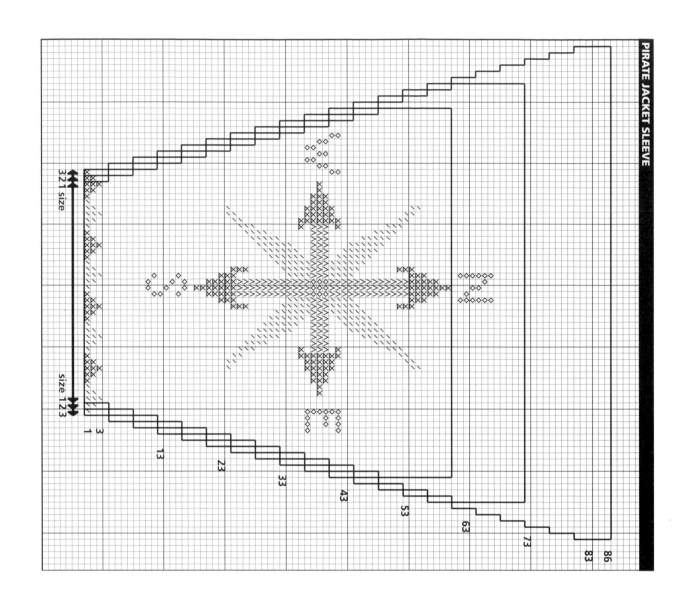

CIRCUS JACKET

SIZES	1	2	3
to fit years	1-2	3-4	5-6
actual chest cm(ins)	65(25½)	76(30)	81(32)
sleeve length cm(ins)	21(8½)	25(10)	32(12½)
back length cm(ins)	30(12)	36(14)	44(17½) (Does not include edging)

MATERIALS
Rowan Handknit Dk cotton 50 g balls

M = turkish plum 277	8	9	10
bleached 263	2	2	2
rosso 215	2	2	2
sunkissed 231	1	1	1
goosebeery 219	1	1	1
flame 254	1	1	1
powder 217	1	1	1
raspberry 240	1	1	1
port 245	1	1	1
basil 221	1	1	1
black 252	1	1	1
fern 364 (chenille)	1	1	1

1 pair each 3¼mm (US 3) and 4 mm (US 5) needles, 5 buttons.

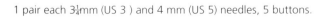

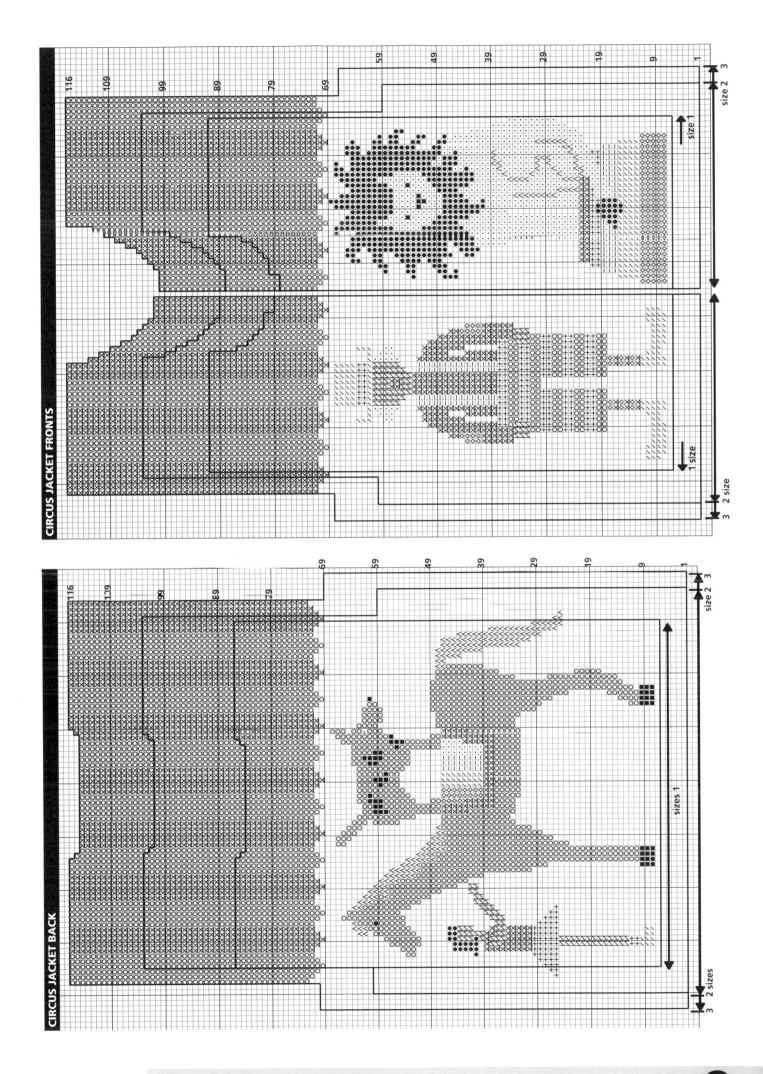

CIRCUS JACKET FRONTS

CIRCUS JACKET BACK

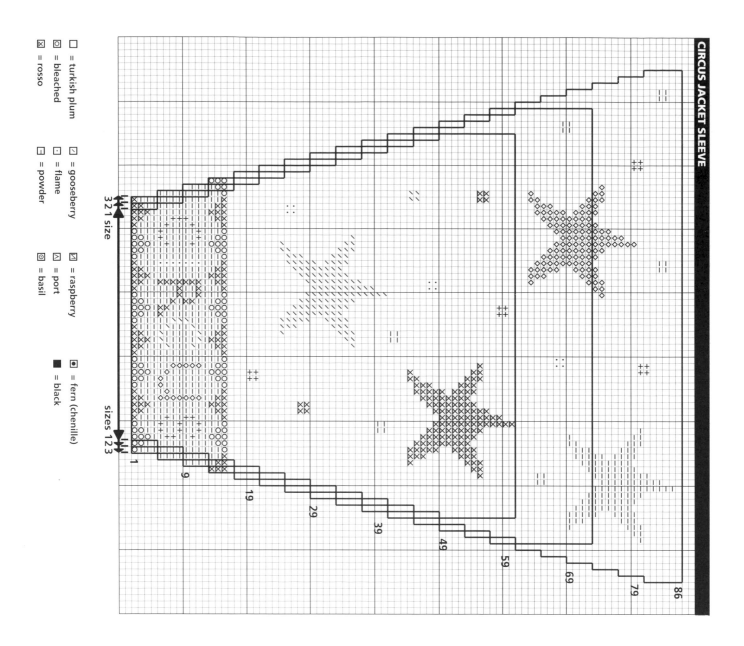

Key:
- ☒ = turkish plum
- ⊡ = bleached
- □ = rosso
- ⊡ = gooseberry
- ⊡ = flame
- ⊡ = powder
- ⊡ = basil
- ⊡ = raspberry
- ⊡ = port
- ⊡ = fern (chenille)
- ■ = black

TENSION
20 sts by 28 rows = 10cm (4ins) square over stocking stitch using 4mm (US 5) needles.

ABBREVIATIONS
see page 80

BACK
Using 4mm (US 5) needles and M cast on 65(76:82) sts and working in stocking stitch follow graph. (Omit girl on size 1 and add 5 more rows before shaping neck.)

FRONTS
Using 4mm (US 5) needles and M cast on 32(38:41) sts and working in stocking stitch follow graph.

SLEEVES
Using 3¼mm (US 3) needles and M cast on 36(38:40) sts and work 6(8:8) rows in moss stitch.
Change to 4mm (US 5) needles and stocking stitch. Follow graph.

POINTED EDGING
Use red, yellow, greens, blue and orange randomly but in complete patt repeats.
Using 4mm (US 5) needles, cast on 2 sts.
Row 1: k2
Row 2: inc, k1
Row 3: k1 p1 inc.
Row 4: inc, k1 p1 k1
Rows 5-8: moss stitch, inc at shaped edge on every row   9 sts
Row 9: moss stitch
Rows 10-16: dec at shaped edge on each row, moss stitch   2 sts
Repeat rows 1-16 until straight edge fits lower edge of garment excluding front bands, ending after a complete patt repeat.

BUTTONBAND
Using 3¼mm (US 3) needles and M cast on 6 sts and work in moss stitch until band, when slightly stretched, fits front to neck shaping. Cast off. Sew into place. Mark positions for 5 buttonholes, the first and last 1cm (½in.) from top and bottom edges and remaining 3 evenly spaced between.

BUTTONHOLE BAND
Work to match buttonband making buttonholes to match button positions by: moss 2, k2tog, yrn, moss 2.

COLLAR
Join shoulder seams. Using 3¼mm (US 3) needles and M, with right side facing and beginning and ending at centre of front bands, pick up and knit 73(77:79) sts from neck. Work as follows:
Rows 1-2: k2, moss to last 2 sts, k2
Row 3: k2, moss to last 3 sts, inc, k2
Repeat row 3 until collar measures 6cm (2¾ins). Cast off loosely in moss stitch.

MAKING UP
Small size: Mark side edges 15cm (6ins) down from shoulder seam. Set sleeves between markers and stitch into place. Join side and sleeve seams. Attach edging. Sew on buttons.
Sizes 2-3: Join side seam. Set in sleeves, placing markers to side seam – see diagram on page 80 – and stitch into place. Join sleeve seam. Attach edging. Sew on buttons.

COLOURED CABLES SWEATER

SIZE (CHILD)	1	2	3	4	5
to fit years	1-2	3-4	5-6	7-8	9-10
actual chest cm(ins)	66(26)	71(28)	76(30)	81(32)	86(34)
back length cm(ins)	33(13)	38(15)	46(18)	49(19)	52(20½)
sleeve seam cm(ins)	22(8½)	28(11)	30(12)	33(13)	35(14)

SIZES (ADULT)	6	7	8
to fit	S	M	L
actual bust cm(ins)	105(41)	112(44)	120(47)
back length cm(ins)	61(24)	61(24)	61(24)
sleeve seam cm(ins)	46(18)	46(18)	46(18)

MATERIALS

Rowan Designer Double Knitting wool 50g balls

SIZES	1	2	3	4	5	6	7	8
M = red 634	5	6	7	8	10	13	14	15
A = light green 435	1	1	1	1	1	1	1	1
B = dark green 685	1	1	1	1	1	2	2	2
C = yellow 610	1	1	1	1	1	2	2	2
D = blue 696	1	1	2	2	2	3	3	3

1 pair each 3¼mm (US 3) and 4mm (US 5) needles, cable needle, stitch holders.

TENSION

24 sts by 32 rows = 10cm (4ins) square over stocking stitch using 3¾mm (US 4) needles.

ABBREVIATIONS

see page 80, and:
c2b = place next st on cable needle, leave at back of work, k1, k1 from cable needle
c2f = place next st on cable needle, leave at front of work, k1, k1 from cable needle
c3b = place next st on cable needle, leave at back of work, k2, k1 from cable needle
c3f = place next 2 sts on cable needle, leave at front of work, k1, k2 from cable needle
c4b = place next 2 sts on cable needle, leave at back of work, k2, k2 from cable needle
c4f = place next 2 sts on cable needle, leave at front of work, k2, k2 from cable needle
c6b = place next 3 sts on cable needle, leave at back of work, k3, k3 from cable needle
c6f = place next 3 sts on cable needle, leave at front of work, k3, k3 from cable needle
x4b = place next st on cable needle, leave at back of work, k3, k1 from cable needle
x4f = place next 3 sts on cable needle, leave at front of work, k1, k3 from cable needle
Bobble = using contrast, k1 yrn k1 into next st, turn; p3, turn; k3, turn; p3, turn; using M, sl k2tog psso; break contrast.

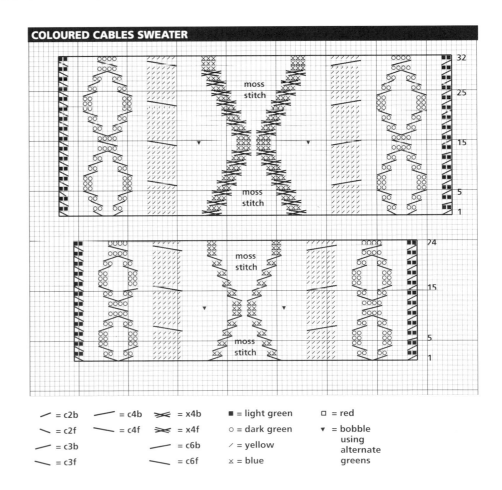

COLOURED CABLES SWEATER

moss stitch

moss stitch

moss stitch

moss stitch

╱ = c2b	╲ = c4b	✕ = x4b
╲ = c2f	╲ = c4f	✕ = x4f
╱ = c3b	╱ = c6b	
╲ = c3f	╲ = c6f	

■ = light green
○ = dark green
╱ = yellow
x = blue

□ = red
▼ = bobble using alternate greens

BACK

Using $3\frac{1}{4}$mm (US 3) needles and M cast on 85(91:97:103:109:129:139:149) sts and work 10(10:10:12:12:16:16:16) rows in moss stitch.

Change to 4mm (US 5) needles and work foundation row as follows:

Work in intarsia (separate yarns for each colour area), not Fairisle.

WS Facing:

Sizes 1-5: moss 8(11:14:17:20) M, purl 2A 5M 4B 5M 6C 5M 2D moss 11M, purl 2D 5M 6C 5M 4B 5M 2A, moss 8(11:14:17:20) M.

Sizes 6-8: moss 25(30:35) M, purl 2A 6M 4B 6M 6C 5M 3D, moss 15M, purl 3D 5M 6C 4B 6M 2A, moss 25(30:35)M.

All sizes: Continue from graph working moss stitch edges with: 69 sts, 24 row repeat for children, or 79 sts, 32 row repeat for adult in stocking stitch for centre panel, until work measures 20(24:31:33:35:40:40:40)cm or 8(9:12:13:14:16:16:16)ins.

Shape armhole: Cast off 4(4:5:5:6:8:9:10) sts beg next 2 rows.

Continue without shaping until work measures 33(38:46:49:52:61:61:61)cm or 13(15:18:19:$20\frac{1}{2}$:24:24:24)ins, ending with RS row, note patt row ***

Shape neck: WS facing: patt 26(28:29:31:32:37:40:43) sts, turn,

Dec neck edge on next 2 rows, cast off.

Place 25(27:29:31:33:39:41:43) sts on holder. Rejoin yarns to remaining sts at neck edge and patt to end. Work * to *.

FRONT

As back to 16(16:18:18:20:24:24:24) rows less than noted row ***

Shape neck: WS facing: patt 32(34:36:38:40:47:51:55) sts turn

**Dec neck edge on next 6(4:6:6:6:6:7:8) rows.

Dec neck edge on alt rows to 24(26:27:29:30:35:38:41) sts.

Work to match back length at shoulder.

Cast off.**

Place 13(15:15:17:17:19:19:19) sts on holder. Rejoin yarns to remaining sts at neck edge, patt to end. Work ** to **.

Cast off.

SLEEVES

Using $3\frac{1}{4}$mm (US 3) needles and M cast on 37(39:41:43:45:51:53:55) sts and work 10(10:10:12:12:16:16:16) rows in moss stitch.

Change to 4mm (US 5) needles and work foundation row as follows:

WS facing: **Sizes 1-5:** p0(1:2:3:4)M, 6C 5M 2D, moss 11M, purl 2D 5M 6C 0(1:2:3:4)M

Sizes 6-8: p4(5:6)M 6C 5M 3D, moss 15M, purl 3D 5M 6C 4(5:6)M.

Continue in patt from graph, inc each end of 3rd and every following 4th row to 69(75:79:85:91:109:109:109) sts.

Continue without shaping until work measures 22(28:30:33:35:46:46:46)cm or $8\frac{1}{2}$(11:12:13:14:18:18:18)ins. Place markers at each end of last row. Work further 5(5:6:6:8:10:11:12) rows. Cast off.

NECKBAND

Join right shoulder seam. With RS facing and using $3\frac{1}{4}$mm (US 3) needles and M, pick up and knit 16(16:18:18:20:24:24:24) sts from side front neck, 13(15:17:17:19:19:19) sts from holder, 16(16:18:18:20:24:24:24) sts from side front neck, 2 sts from side back neck, 25(27:29:31:33:39:41:43) sts from holder and 2 sts from side back neck.

Work 9(9:9:9:11:13:13:13) rows in moss stitch. Cast off loosely in moss stitch.

MAKING UP

Join left shoulder seam and neckband. Join side seams. Set in sleeve head, markers to side seam (see diagram on page 80) and stitch into position. Join sleeve seam. Weave in any loose ends.

COLOURED CABLES HAT

SIZES	**1**	**2**	**3**	**4**
to fit	1-3yrs	4-6 yrs	7-10 yrs	Adult

MATERIALS

Rowan Designer Double Knitting wool 50g balls				
M = blue 696	1	1	2	2
A = yellow 610	1	1	1	1
B = red 634	1	1	1	1
C = green 635	1	1	1	1

1 pair each $3\frac{1}{4}$mm(US 3) and $3\frac{3}{4}$mm (US 4) needles, cable needle.

TENSION

24 sts by 32 rows = 10cm (4ins) square over stocking stitch using $3\frac{3}{4}$mm (US 4) needles.

ABBREVIATIONS

see page 80, and:

c6b = place next 3 sts on cable needle, leave at back of work, k3, k3 from cable needle

METHOD

Using $3\frac{1}{4}$mm (US 3) needles and M cast on 108(120:132:144) sts and work 6(7:9:10)cms or $2\frac{1}{2}$(3:$3\frac{1}{2}$:4)ins in k1 p1 rib.

Change to 3mm (US 4) needles and work as follows:

Row 1: knit *6(7:8:9)M 6A 12(14:16:18)M 6B 12(14:16:18)M 6C 6(7:8:9)M* twice

Row 2: purl *6(7:8:9)M 6C 12(14:16:18)M 6B 12(14:16:18)M 6A 6(7:8:9)M* twice

Row 3-4: as rows 1 and 2.

Row 5: knit *6(7:8:9)M c6bA 12(14:16:18)M c6bB 12(14:16:18)M c6bC 6(7:8:9)M* twice.

Row 6: as row 2

Rows 1-6 form patt repeat. Continue in patt until work measures 18(20:22:24)cm or $7\frac{1}{4}$(8:$8\frac{3}{4}$:$9\frac{1}{2}$)ins.

Shape crown: Keeping cables correct:

Row 1:*k4(5:6:7) k2tog, patt 6, s1 k1 psso k4(5:6:7)* 6 times *96(108:120:132) sts*

Row 2-4: patt

Row 5: *k3(4:5:6) k2tog, patt 6, s1 k1 psso k3(4:5:6)* 6 times ***84(96:108:120) sts***

Row 6-8: patt

Size 1

Row 9: *k2 k2tog, patt 6, s1 k1 psso k2* 6 times

Row 10: [p3 *p2tog* 3 times, p3] 6 times

Row 11: *k2tog* to end.

Size 2

Row 9: *k3 k2tog, patt 6, s1 k1 psso k3* 6 times

Row 10: patt

Row 11-13: as rows 9-11 of size 1

Size 3

Row 9: *k4 k2tog, patt 6, s1 k1 psso k4* 6 times

Row 10-12: patt

Row 13-17: as rows 9-13 of size 2

Size 4

Row 9: *k5 k2tog, patt 6, s1 k1 psso k5* 6 times

Row 10-12: patt

Row 13-21: as row 9-17 of size 3

MAKING UP

Break yarns leaving a long sewing thread. Pass thread through remaining sts, pull tightly and secure. Stitch back seam. Weave in any loose ends. Make pom-pom and attach to centre of crown.

KELIM JACKET

Size	1	2
to fit cm(ins)	92-99 (36-38)	100-107(39-42)
actual bust cm(ins)	112(44)	120(47)
back length cm(ins)	69(27)	69(27)
sleeve seam cm(ins)	43(17)	43(17)

MATERIALS

Rowan Designer Double Knitting wool 50g balls

	1	2
M = blue 696	10	11
pink 634	2	2
orange 699	2	2
yellow 610	2	2
lime green 635	2	2
dark green 685	2	2
turquoise 609	2	2

1 pair each 3¼mm (US 3) and 3¾mm (US 4) needles, stitch holders, 6 buttons.

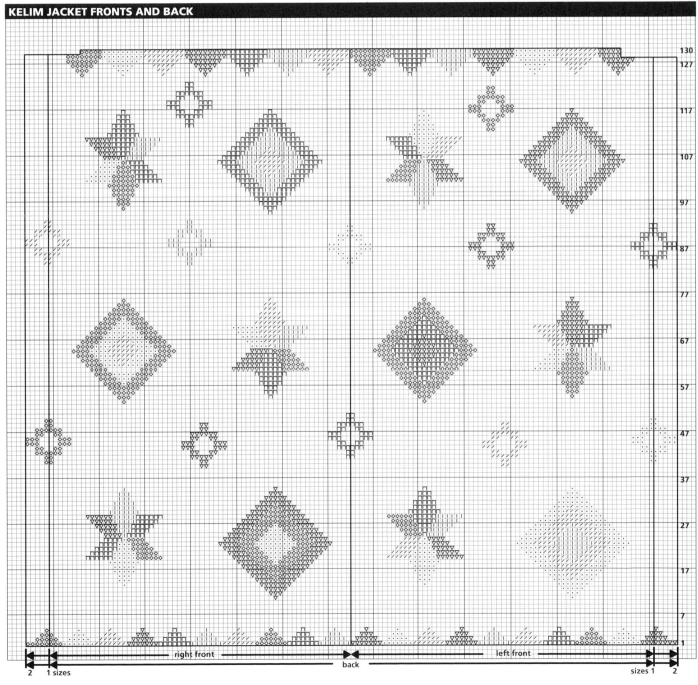

KELIM JACKET FRONTS AND BACK

right front   back   left front

2 1 sizes   sizes 1 2

130
127
117
107
97
87
77
67
57
47
37
27
17
7
1

Note: Left sleeve: start with a knit row.   Right sleeve: start with purl row.

key
□ = blue
⊠ = pink
□ = orange   ⊠ = yellow
□ = lime green   □ = turquoise
□ = dark green

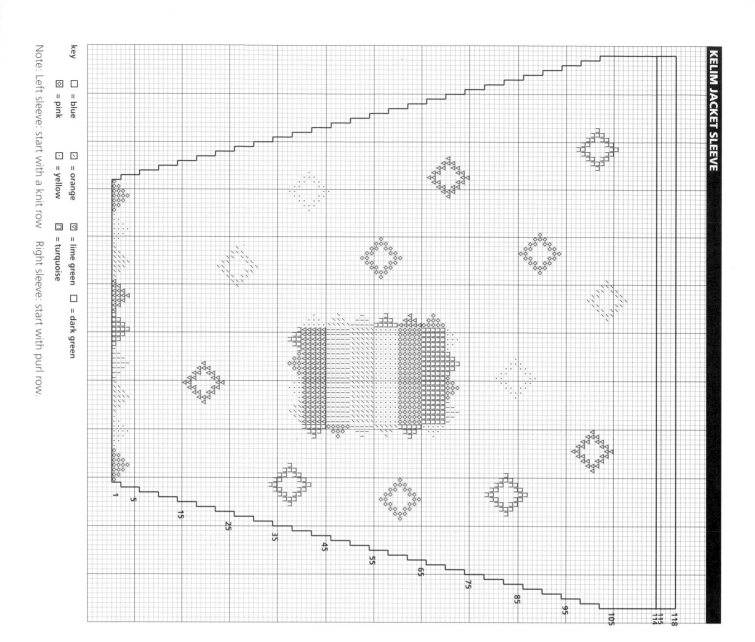

TENSION
24 sts by 32 rows = 10cm (4ins) square over stocking stitch using 3¾mm (US 4) needles.

ABBREVIATIONS
see page 80

BACK
Using 3¼mm (US 3) needles and M cast on 132(142) sts and work 12 rows in moss stitch. Change to 3¾mm (US 4) needles and stocking stitch. Work rows 1-130 from graph. Continue in stripes as set until completion of row 212.
Row 213: **Shape neck:** patt 42, cast off 34 sts, patt 42
On 42 sts, dec neck edge on next 3 rows. Cast off.
Rejoin yarn to remaining sts at neck edge and work to match.

POCKETS (2)
Using 3¾mm (US 4) needles and M cast on 24 sts and work 30 rows in stocking stitch. Leave on holder.

LEFT FRONT
Using 3¼mm (US 3) needles and M cast on 66(71) sts and work 12 rows in moss stitch. Change to 3¾mm (US 4) needles and stocking stitch. Work rows 1-130 from graph, **noting** row 31: place pocket, patt 21(26), place next 24 sts on holder, patt across 24 sts of pocket, patt to end. Continue in stripes to completion of row 191.
Row 192: **Shape neck:** cast off 5 sts, patt to end
Row 193: patt
Row 194: cast off 3 sts, patt to end
Row 195-200: dec neck edge, patt
Row 201-212: dec neck edge on alt rows
39 sts
Row 213-216: patt
Cast off.

RIGHT FRONT
As left front to completion of row 191, **noting** row 31: patt 21, place next 24 sts on holder, patt across 24 sts of pocket, patt to end.
Row 192: patt
Row 193: **Shape neck:** Cast off 5 sts, patt to end
Row 194: patt
Row 195: cast off 3 sts, patt to end
Row 196-201: dec neck edge, patt
Row 202-213: dec neck edge on alt rows (39 sts)
Row 214-216: patt
Cast off.

SLEEVES (Left)
Using 3¼mm (US 3) needles and M cast on 63 sts and work 6cm (2½ins) in moss stitch. Change to 3¾mm (US 4) needles and stocking stitch. Follow graph, starting with a knit row.

(Right)
Cuff as left sleeve.
Change to 3¾mm(US 4) needles and stocking stitch. Follow graph, starting with a purl row.

BUTTONBAND
Using 3¼mm (US 3) needles and M cast on 11 sts and work in moss stitch until band when slightly stretched fits left front edge. Cast off and stitch into place.

BUTTONHOLE BAND

As buttonband but add 6 buttonholes, the first to come 1cm (½in) from cast-on edge, the last 1cm (½in) from cast-off edge and the 4 others equally spaced along band. Stitch into place.
Buttonhole: Row 1: moss 5, cast off 2 sts, moss 4
Row 2: moss 4, cast on 2 sts, moss 5.

POCKET TOPS

Using 3¾mm (US 3) needles and M work 7 rows in moss stitch. Cast off in moss stitch.

COLLAR

Join shoulder seams.
Using 3¾mm (US 3) needles and M pick up 113 sts around neck, starting and finishing halfway across front bands. Work as follows:
Row 1-2: k2, moss to last 2 sts, k2

Row 3: k2, moss to last 3 sts, inc, k2
Repeat row 3 until work measures 8cm (3¼ins). Cast off loosely in moss stitch.

MAKING UP

Join side seams. Slipstitch pockets and pocket tops into position. Set in sleeve head having marker at side seam (see diagram on page 80). Stitch into place. Join sleeve seam. Weave in any loose ends. Sew on buttons.

STRIPY MOSS-STITCH SWEATER

SIZES (CHILD)	1	2	3	4	5
to fit loosely years	1-2	3-4	5-6	7-8	9-10
actual chest cm(ins)	66(26)	69(27)	72(28)	75(29½)	80(31)
back length cm(ins)	33(13)	38(15)	46(18)	50(19½)	54(21)
sleeve seam cm(ins)	22(8½)	28(11)	30(12)	33(13)	35(14)

SIZES (ADULT)	6	7	8
to fit	S	M	L
actual bust cm(ins)	105(41)	112(44)	120(47)
back length cm(ins)	69(27)	69(27)	69(27)
sleeve seam cm(ins)	46(18)	46(18)	46(18)

MATERIALS	1	2	3	4	5
Rowan Magpie Aran wool 100g hanks					
speedwell 508	1	1	1	2	2
turq 308	1	1	1	2	2
rocket 509	1	1	1	1	1
pumice 301	1	1	1	1	1
peony 306	1	1	1	1	1

MATERIALS	6	7	8
Rowan Magpie Aran Wool 100g			
speedwell 508	3	3	3
turq 308	2	2	3
rocket 509	2	2	2
pumice 301	2	2	2
peony 306	2	2	2

1 pair each 3¾mm (US 4) and 4½mm (US 6) needles, stitch holders.

TENSION

20 sts by 26 rows = 10cm (4ins) square over stocking stitch using 4½mm (US 6) needles.

ABBREVIATIONS

see page 80

BACK

Using 3¾mm (US 4) needles and speedwell cast on 63(67:71:75:79:93:99:105) sts and work 8(8:8:10:10:12:12:12) rows in moss stitch.
Change to 4½mm (US 6) needles and work in stripe patt in moss stitch as follows:
*Rows 1- 8: speedwell
Rows 9-24 : turq
Rows 25-40: rocket
Rows 41-56: pumice

Rows 57-72: peony
Rows 73-80: speedwell*
Rows 1-80 form patt repeat.
Work in patt until back measures 19(24:30:33:35:46:46:46)cm or 7½(9½:12: 13:14:18:18:18)ins.
Shape armhole: Cast off 3(3:4:4:4:5:5:5) sts beg next 2 rows.
Cont without shaping until work measures 33(38:46:50:54:69:69:69)cm or 13(15:18:19½:21:27:27:27)ins.
** Note patt row.
Shape neck: patt 19(20:21:22:23:28:31: 33) sts, turn
Dec neck edge on next 2 rows. Cast off in moss stitch.
Place centre 19(21:21:23:25:27:27:27) sts on holder.
Rejoin yarn to remaining sts at neck edge,

patt to end.
Work * to *.

FRONT

As back to 14(14:16:16:16:18:18:18) rows less than ** noted row.
Shape neck: patt 24(26:26:28:30:35:38: 41) sts, turn
*Dec neck edge on next 5(4:4:4:6:6:6) rows.
Dec neck edge on alt rows to 17(18:19:20: 21:26:29:31) sts.
Cont to match back at shoulder. Cast off.*
Place centre 9(9:11:11:11:13:13:13) sts on holder. Rejoin yarn to remaining sts at neck edge and patt to end. Work * to *.

SLEEVES

Using 3¾mm (US 4) needles and speedwell cast on 31(33:35:37:39:49:49:49) sts and work 8(8:8:10:10:12:12:12) rows in moss stitch. Change to 4½mm (US 6) needles and stripe patt as on back. Inc each end of row 3 and every following 5(5:5:5:5:4:4: 4) row to 51(59:61:63:65:91:91:91) sts.
Continue without shaping until work measures 22(28:30:33:35:46:46:46)cm or 8½(11:12:13:14:18:18:18)ins. Place markers at ends of last row. Work 4(4:5:5: 5:6:6:6) more rows. Cast off in moss stitch.

NECKBAND

Join right shoulder seam. With RS facing and using 3¾mm (US 4) needles and speedwell pick up and knit 14(14:16:16: 16:18:18:18) sts from side front neck, 9(9:11:11:11:13:13:13) sts from holder, 14(14:16:16:16:18:18:18) sts from side front neck, 2 sts from side back neck, 19(21:21:23:25:27:27:27) sts from holder and 2 sts from side back neck.
Work 4(5:5:6:6:8:8:8) rows in moss stitch.
Cast off in moss stitch.

MAKING UP

Join left shoulder seam and neckband. Join side seams. Set in sleeve head, markers to side seam (see diagram on page 80). Stitch into position. Join sleeve seams. Weave in any loose ends.

HEARTS SWEATER

SIZES	1	2	3	4	5
to fit years	1-2	3-4	5-6	7-8	9-10
actual chest cm(ins)	71(28)	77(30)	84(33)	89(35)	94(37)
back length cm(ins)	33(13)	38(15)	46(18)	51(20)	56(22)
sleeve seam cm(ins)	22(8½)	28(11)	30(12)	33(13)	35(14)

MATERIALS

Rowan Cotton Glace 50g balls

delft 782	3	4	5	6	6
sky 749	1	1	2	2	2
parade 430	1	1	2	2	2
kiwi 443	1	1	2	2	2
banana 444	1	1	2	2	2
terracotta 786	1	1	2	2	2
carnival 4323	1	1	2	2	2
bubblegum 441	1	1	2	2	2

1 pair each 2¾mm (US 1) and 3¼mm (US 3) needles, stitch holders.

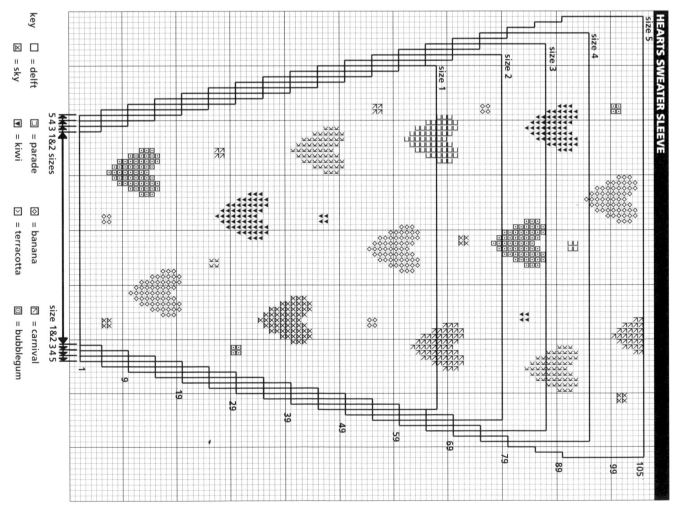

key

☐ = delft
☒ = sky
▣ = parade
▼ = kiwi
☑ = banana
◙ = terracotta
▨ = carnival
▣ = bubblegum

543182 sizes

size 1&2345

HEARTS SWEATER SLEEVE

size 1
size 2
size 3
size 4
size 5

5 4 3 2 1 sizes   back and front   sizes 1 2 3 4 5

Hearts sweater   **67**

TENSION
23 sts by 32 rows = 10cm (4ins) square over stocking stitch using 3¼mm (US 3) needles.

ABBREVIATIONS
see page 80

BACK AND FRONT
Using 2¾mm (US 1) needles and delft cast on 83(89:95:101:107) sts and work 12 rows in moss stitch. Change to 3¼mm (US 3) needles and stocking stitch. Follow graph, leaving centre neck stitches on holders.

SLEEVES
Using 2¾mm (US 1) needles and carnival cast on 39(39:41:43:45) sts and work 6(16:16:16:16) rows in moss stitch. Change to 3¼mm (US 3) needles and stocking stitch. Follow graph, placing marker at * on graph.

NECKBAND
Join right shoulder seam. Using 2¾mm (US 1) needles and delft, with RS facing, pick up and knit 16(16:18:18:20) sts from side front neck, 13(15:15:17:17) sts from centre front neck, 16(16:18:18:20) sts from side front neck, 2 sts from side back neck, 25(27:29:31:33) sts from centre back neck and 2 sts from side back neck. Work 7(7:7:9:9) rows in moss stitch. Cast off loosely in moss stitch.

MAKING UP
Join left shoulder seam and neckband. Join side seams. Set in sleeve head, marker to side seam (see diagram on page 80) and stitch into place. Join sleeve seams. Weave in any loose ends.

DOLLY MIXTURE WAISTCOAT

Sizes	1	2	3	4	5
to fit years	1-2	3-4	5-6	7-8	9-10
actual chest cm(ins)	56(22)	61(24)	66(26)	71(28)	76(30)
back length cm(ins)	31(12)	35(14)	40(16)	43(17)	46(18)

MATERIALS
Rowan Cotton Glace 50g balls

	1	2	3	4	5
M = parade 430	3	3	4	4	5
A = terracotta 786	1	1	1	1	1
B = bubblegum 441	1	1	1	1	1
C = carnival 432	1	1	1	1	1
D = delft 782	1	1	1	1	1
E = sky 749	1	1	1	1	1
F = banana 444	1	1	1	1	1
G = kiwi 443	1	1	1	1	1

1 pair each 2¾mm (US 1) and 3¼mm (US 3) needles, 4 buttons.

TENSION
23 sts by 32 rows = 10cm (4ins) square over stocking stitch using 3¼mm (US 3) needles.

ABBREVIATIONS
see page 80

BACK
Using 2¾mm (US 1) needles and M cast on 65(71:77:83:89) sts and work 10 rows in moss stitch.
Change to 3¼mm (US 3) needles and stocking stitch. Work in stripe patt of 4 rows A, B, C, D, E, F, G and M (32 row repeat). Cont to completion of row 42(54:66:74:82).
Keeping patt correct, **shape armhole:** Cast off 3(4:3:4:4) sts beg next 2 rows, then:
Sizes 1(2)
Dec each end of every row to 49(57) sts.
Dec each end of alt rows to 47(51) sts.
Sizes 3(4:5)
Cast off 3(3:4) sts beg next 2 rows.
Dec each end of every row to 57(61:67) sts
Dec each end of alt rows to 53(57:61) sts
All sizes
Cont without shaping to completion of row 86(100:114:124:134).
Shape shoulders and neck:
Row 1: Cast off 6(6:6:7:7) sts, patt 10(12:12:12:13) sts, cast off 15(15:17:19:21) sts, patt to end
Row 2: Cast off 6(6:6:7:7) sts, patt to end
Row 3: Cast off 4(5:5:5:5) sts, patt to end
Row 4: Cast off
Rejoin yarn to remaining sts at neck edge and work rows 3-4.

LEFT AND RIGHT FRONTS
Using 2¾mm (US 1) needles and M cast on 32(35:38:41:44) sts and work 10 rows in moss stitch.
Change to 3¼mm (US 3) needles and stocking stitch. Follow graph.

ARMBANDS
Join shoulder seams. Using 2¾mm (US 1) needles and M pick up and knit 73(77:85:89:95) sts around armhole. Work 5 rows in moss stitch. Cast off in moss stitch.

BUTTONBAND
Using 2¾mm (US 1) needles and M cast on 6 sts and work in moss stitch. Make 4 buttonholes, placing the first 1cm (½in) from cast on, the 4th at start of V-shaping and the other 2 evenly spaced between.
To make buttonhole:
Row 1: moss 2, cast off 2 sts, moss 2
Row 2: moss 2, cast on 2 sts, moss 2
Cont with band until it fits around front edge. Cast off.

MAKING UP
Join side seams. Attach front band. Sew in any loose ends. Sew on buttons.

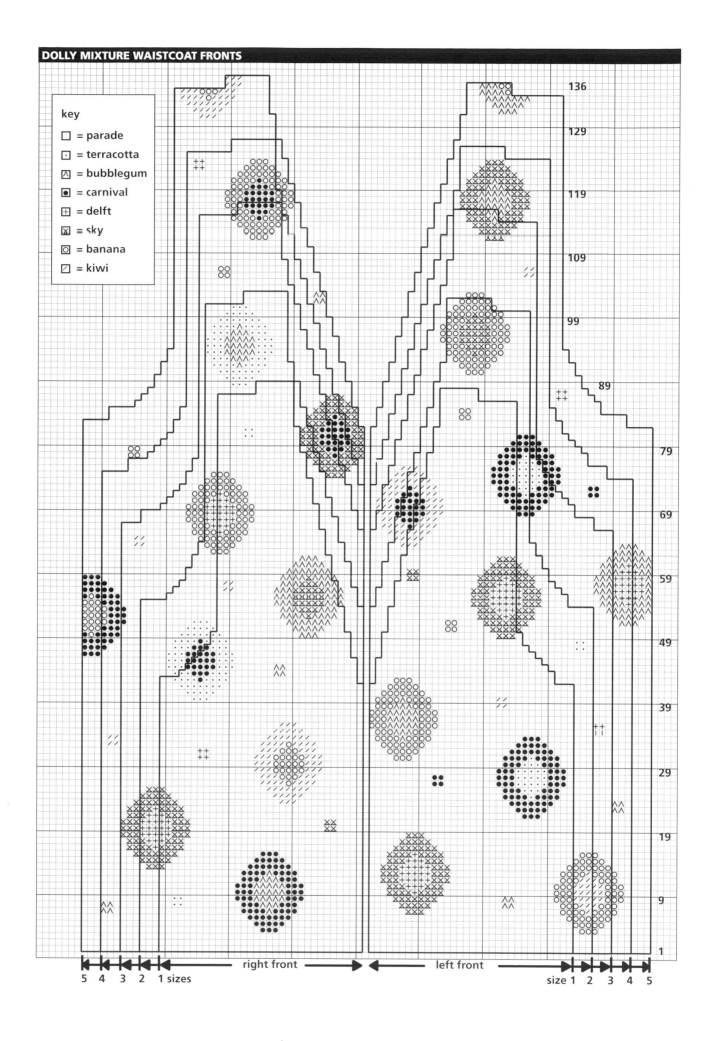

key

□ = parade
⊡ = terracotta
⊠ = bubblegum
⬤ = carnival
⊞ = delft
⊠ = sky
⊙ = banana
⧄ = kiwi

136
129
119
109
99
89
79
69
59
49
39
29
19
9
1

right front → ← left front →

5 4 3 2 1 sizes   size 1 2 3 4 5

MEXICAN SWEATER AND JACKET

Jacket for child only; sizes 6 and 7 are adult sizes

SIZES	1	2	3	6	7
to fit years	1-2	3-4	5-6	S-M	M-L
actual chest cm(ins)	66(26)	80(31½)	84(33)	109(43)	119(47)
back length cm(ins)	31(12)	38(15)	46(18)	61(24)	61(24)
sleeve seam cm(ins)	20(8)	25(10)	30(12)	44(17½)	44(17½)

MATERIALS
Rowan Handknit Dk cotton 50g balls

M = powder 217	6	8	9	13	14
A = sailor blue 232	1	2	2	4	4
B = basil 321	1	1	1	1	1
C = summer pudding 243	1	1	1	1	1
D = sunkissed 231	1	1	1	1	1
E = flame 254	1	1	1	1	1
black 252	1	1	1	1	1
bleached 263	2	2	2	3	3

NOTE:
The above colours are for the adult colourway. For the green children's jacket, please change:
M = basil 321, A = turkish plum 277,
B = popcorn 229, C = rosso 215,
D = aqua 220, E = flame 254; black 252 and bleached 263 for the borders.
For the red children's sweater please change M = rosso 215, A = turkish plum 277, B = basil 321, C = lime 234,
D = popcorn 229, E = flame 254; black 252 and bleached 263 for the borders.

1 pair each 3mm (US 2) and 4mm (US 5) needles, stitch holders (sweater only), 5 buttons (jacket only)

TENSION
20 sts by 28 rows = 10cm (4ins) square over stocking stitch using 4mm (US 5) needles.

ABBREVIATIONS
see page 80

SWEATER

BACK
Using 3mm (US 2) needles and A cast on 65(79:85:109:119) sts and work 10 rows in moss stitch.
Change to 4mm (US 5) needles and stocking stitch. Follow graph for border (rows 1-15) then repeat rows 16-44, using contrasts randomly and ensuring that the same colours are not adjacent, until work measures 17(23:30:38:38)cm or 6¾(9:12: 15:15)ins.
Shape armhole: cast off 3(4:4:5:5) sts beg next 2 rows.
Cont until work measures 31(38:46:61: 61)cm or 12(15:18:24:24)ins ending with RS row.
Note patt row ***

Shape neck: patt 19(24:26:31:36) sts turn
dec neck edge on next 2 rows. Cast off.
Place centre 21(23:25:37:37) sts on holder.
Rejoin yarns to remaining sts at neck edge and patt to end.
Work * to * again.

FRONT
As back to 11(13:15:21:21) rows less than *** on back.
Shape neck: RS facing:
patt 25(31:34:43:48) sts turn
**dec neck edge on next 6(6:6:8:8) rows dec neck edge on alt rows to 17(22:24:29: 34) sts.
Work to match back length at shoulder. Cast off.**
Place centre 9(9:9:13:13) sts on holder.
Rejoin yarns to remaining sts at neck edge and patt to end.
Work ** to **.

MEXICAN SWEATER AND JACKET FRONTS AND BACK

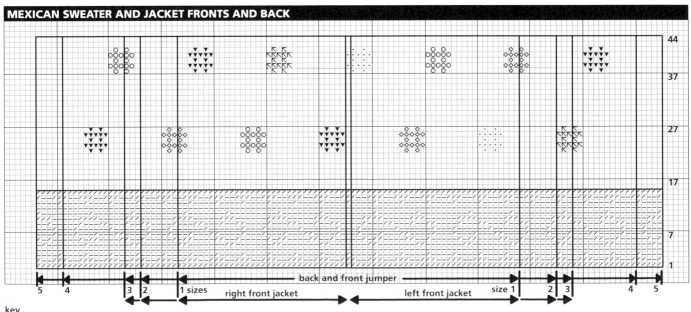

key
adult colourway ☐ = powder ☒ = black ☐ = bleached **other symbols use colours randomly**

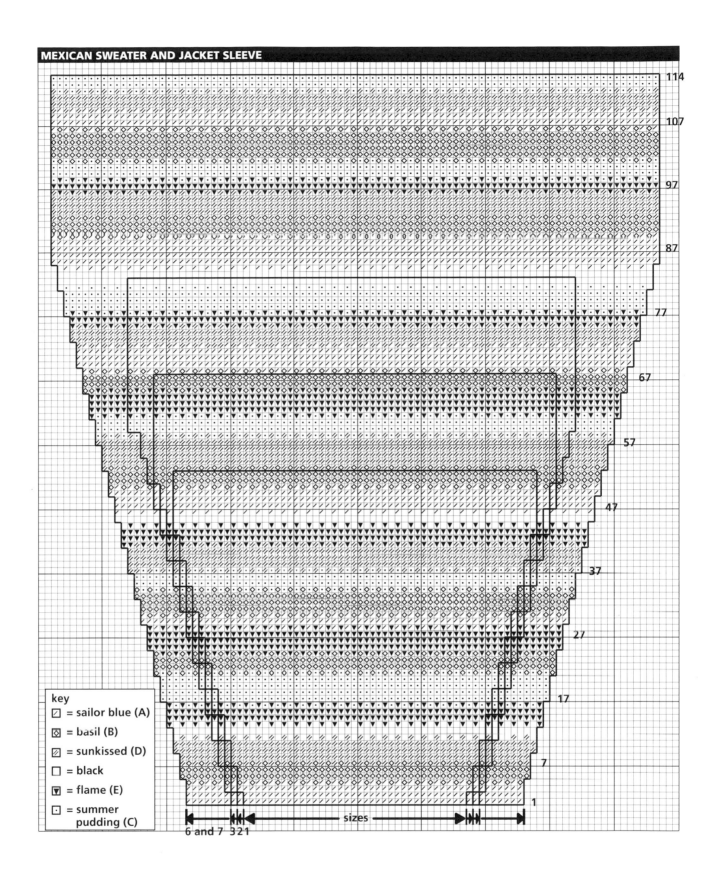

key
☑ = sailor blue (A)
◙ = basil (B)
☑ = sunkissed (D)
☐ = black
▼ = flame (E)
⚬ = summer pudding (C)

SLEEVES

Using 3mm (US 2) needles and A cast on 35(37:39:47:47) sts. Work 10(10:10:9:9) rows in moss stitch.

Row 10: **sizes 6 and 7:** moss 3 *inc, moss 7* 5 times, inc moss 3   *53 sts*
Change to 4mm (US 5) needles and stocking stitch. Follow graph.

NECKBAND

Join right shoulder seam. With RS facing and using 3mm (US 2) needles and M pick up and knit 14(16:18:24:24) sts from side front neck, 9(9:9:13:13) sts from holder, 14(16:18:24:24) sts from side front neck, 3(4:3:3:3) sts from side back neck 21(23:25:37:37) sts from holder,3(4:3:3:3) sts from side back neck.Work as folls,keeping all floats to WS of work.
Row 1: *k2M p2A* to end

Row 2: *k2A p2M* to end
Sizes 1, 2 and 3: repeat rows 1 and 2 twice more.
Adult sizes 6 and 7: repeat rows 1 and 2 three times more.
All sizes: next row using A *k2 p* to end. Cast off in A.

MAKING UP

Join left shoulder seam and side seams. Set in sleeve head, markers to side seam (see

Mexican sweater and jacket

diagram on page 80), stitch into place. Join sleeve seams. Weave in any loose ends.

JACKET
Sizes 1, 2 and 3 only
Back as for jumper to note patt row ***
Shape neck: patt 21(26:28), cast off 17(19:21) sts, patt 21(26:28)
dec neck edge on next 2 rows. Cast off.
Rejoin yarns to remaining sts at neck edge and work to match.

LEFT FRONT
Using 3mm (US 2) needles and A cast 32(39:42) sts and work 10 rows in moss stitch.
Change to 4mm (US 5) needles and stocking stitch. Follow graph for border (rows 1-15) then repeat rows 16-45 as on back until work measures 17(23:30)cm or 6¾(9:12) ins.
Shape armhole: RS facing, cast off 3(4:4) sts, patt to end.
Cont until work is 10(12:12) rows less than *** on back.
Shape neck: WS facing: *cast off 4(5:5) sts, patt to end. Dec neck edge on next 2(3:4) rows.
Dec neck edge on alt rows to 19(24:26) sts. Work to match back at shoulder. Cast off.*

RIGHT FRONT
As left front to armhole. Work 1 row.
Shape armhole: WS facing: cast off 3(4:4) sts, patt to end.
Cont to 9(11:11) rows less than *** on back. **Shape neck** as for left front starting RS facing.

SLEEVES
As for jumper.

BUTTONBAND
With 3mm (US 2) needles and A cast on 6 sts and work in moss stitch until band, when slightly stretched, fits front edge to neck shaping. Cast off. Sew into place. Mark positions for 5 buttons, the first and last 1cm (½in) from top and bottom and the remaining 3 evenly spaced between.

BUTTONHOLE BAND
As buttonband but make buttonholes to match marked positions by:
moss 2, k2tog, yrn, moss 2.

COLLAR
Join shoulder seams. With RS facing and using 3mm (US 2) needles and A pick up and knit 73(77:79) sts around neck, starting and finishing at centre of front bands. Work as folls:
Rows 1 and 2: k2, moss to last 2 sts, k2
Row 3: k2, moss to last 3 sts, inc, k2
Repeat row 3 until work measures 6cm (2½ins). Cast off loosely in moss stitch.

MAKING UP
Join side seams. Set in sleeve head, markers to side seam (see diagram on page 80), stitch into position. Join sleeve seams. Weave in any loose ends. Sew on buttons.

CHILD'S DENIM SWEATER

SIZES	1	2	3	4	5
to fit years	1-2	3-4	5-6	7-8	9-10
actual chest cm(ins)	68(26½)	76(30)	84(33)	89(35)	94(37)
back length cm(ins)	33(13)	38(15)	46(18)	51(20)	56(22)

MATERIALS
Rowan denim Dk cotton 50g balls

SIZES	1	2	3	4	5
	7	8	9	10	10

1 pair each 3¼mm (US 3) and 4mm (US 5) needles, cable needle, stitch holder

TENSION
20 sts by 28 rows = 10cm (4ins) square over stocking stitch using 4mm (US 5) needles.

ABBREVIATIONS
see page 80, and:
c2b = place next st on cable needle, leave at back of work, k1, k1 from cable needle
c2f = place next st on cable needle, leave at front of work, k1, k1 from cable needle
c3b = place next st on cable needle, leave at back of work k2, k1 from cable needle
c3f = place next 2 sts on cable needle, leave at front of work, k1, k2 from cable needle
c4b = place next 2 sts on cable needle, leave at back of work, k2, k2 from cable needle
c4f = place next 2 sts on cable needle, leave at front of work, k2, k2 from cable needle
t2b = place next st on cable needle, leave at back of work, k1, p1 from cable needle
t2f = place next st on cable needle, leave at front of work, p1, k1 from cable needle
t3b = place next st on cable needle, leave at back of work, k2, p1 from cable needle
t3f = place next 2 sts on cable needle, leave at front of work, p1, k2 from cable needle
x3b = place next st on cable needle, leave at back of work, k2, k1 from cable needle (work this instruction on a WS row)
x3f = place next 2 sts on cable needle, leave at front of work, k1, k2 from cable needle (work this instruction on a WS row)

Note: Garment will appear over long and loosely knitted. It must be shrunk to size by washing (see Making Up) and will shrink approximately ⅕th in length.

BACK
Using 3mm (US 3) needles cast on 67(75:83:89:95) sts and work 7(9:9:11:11) rows in moss stitch.
Next row: moss 24(28:32:35:38) sts, *inc, moss 9* twice, inc moss to end
70(78:86:92:98) sts.
Change to 4mm (US 5) needles and graph, continue until work measures 40(45:54:61:67)cm or 15¾(17¾:21¼:24:

26¼)ins. *** note patt row.
Shape neck: patt 25(28:31:33:35) sts, turn *dec neck edge on next 2 rows. Cast off.*
Place centre 20(22:24:26:28) sts on holder. Rejoin yarn to remaining sts at neck edge and patt to end. Work * to *.

FRONT
As back to 16(18:20:22:24) rows less than *** on back.
Shape neck: patt 28(32:35:38:40) sts turn *dec neck edge on next 2(3:3:4:4) rows. Dec neck edge on alt rows to 23(26:29:31:33) sts. Cont to match back length at shoulder. Cast off.*
Place centre 14(14:16:16:18) sts on holder rejoin yarn to remaining sts at neck edge, patt to end. Work * to *.

SLEEVES

Using 3¼mm (US 3) needles cast on 33(35:37:39:41) sts and work 7(9:9:11:11) rows in moss stitch.
Next row: moss 6(7:8:9:10) *inc, moss 9* twice, inc, moss to end

36(38:40:42:44) sts.

Change to 4mm (US 5) needles and patt as folls:
moss 5(6:7:8:9), p1 k4 p2 k2, moss 8, k2 p2 k4 p1, moss 5(6:7:8:9).
Cont as set, working 4 sts cables and centre panel with moss stitch edges, inc each end of 3rd and every foll 4th row to 58(62:66:72:76) sts. Cont without shaping

until work measures 26(33:36:40:42)cm or 10¼(13:14:15¾:16½)ins. Cast off.

NECK BAND

Join right shoulder seam. With RS facing and using 3¼mm (US 3) needles pick up and knit 18(20:22:24:26) sts from side front neck, 14(14:16:16:18) sts from centre front neck, 18(20:22:24:26) sts from side front neck, 3 sts from side back neck, 20(22:24:26:28) sts from centre back neck and 3 sts from side back neck. Work 7(7:7:9:9) rows in moss stitch. Cast off loosely in moss stitch .

MAKING UP

Join neck band and left shoulder seam. Set in sleeves and stitch into place. Join side and sleeve seams. Weave in any loose ends. To shrink, wash in hot wash and tumble dry.

Note: The beauty of denim yarn is that it will fade with every wash as jeans do, enhancing the cables.

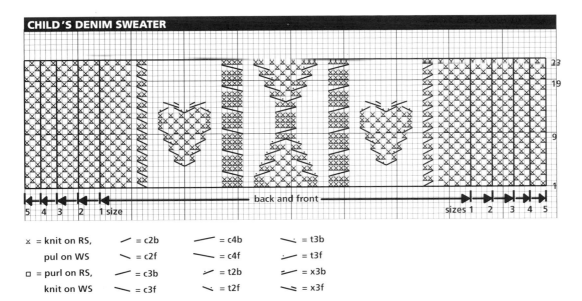

CHILD'S DENIM SWEATER

| x = knit on RS, pul on WS | ╱ = c2b ╲ = c2f | ╱ = c4b ╲ = c4f | ╲ = t3b ╱ = t3f |
| □ = purl on RS, knit on WS | ╱ = c3b ╲ = c3f | ╱ = t2b ╲ = t2f | ╱ = x3b ╲ = x3f |

back and front

5 4 3 2 1 size   sizes 1 2 3 4 5

ADULT'S DENIM SWEATER

SIZES

	M	L
actual bust cm (ins)	112(44)	122(48)
back length cm(ins)	68(26½)	68(26½)
sleeve seam cm(ins)	46(18)	46(18)

MATERIALS

Rowan Denim Dk cotton 50g balls		
	18	20

1 pair each 3¼mm (US 3) and 4mm(US 5) needles, cable needle, stitch holders

TENSION

20 sts by 28 rows = 10cm (4ins) square over stocking stitch using 4mm (US 5) needles.

ABBREVIATIONS

see page 80 and:
c2f = place next st on cable needle, leave at front, k1, k1 from cable needle
c2b = place next st on cable needle, leave at back, k1, k1 from cable needle
x3f = place next 2 sts on cable needle, leave at front, k1, k2 from cable needle (worked on a wrong side row)
x3b = place next st on cable needle, leave at back, k2, k1 from cable needle (worked on a wrong side row)
t3f = place next 2 sts on cable needle,

leave at front of work, p1, k2 from cable needle
t3b = place next st on cable needle, leave at back of work, k2, p1 from cable needle
c3f = place next 2 sts on cable needle, leave at front of work, k1, k2 from cable needle
c3b = place next st on cable needle, leave at back of work, k2, k1 from cable needle
t4f = place next 2 sts on cable needle, leave at front of work, p2, k2 from cable needle
t4b = place next 2 sts on cable needle, leave at back of work, k2, p2 from cable needle
c4f = place next 2 sts on cable needle, leave at front of work, k2, k2 from cable needle
c4b = place next 2 sts on cable needle, leave at back of work, k2, k2 from cable needle
c6f = place next 3 sts on cable needle, leave

at front of work, k3, k3 from cable needle
c6b = place next 3 sts on cable needle, leave at back of work, k3, k3 from cable needle.

Note: Garment will appear over long and loosely knitted. It must be shrunk to size by washing (see Making Up) and will shrink approximately ⅕th in length.

BACK

Using 3¼mm (US 3) needles cast on 122 (136) sts and work as follows:
Row 1: p3 *k4 p3* to end
Row 2: k3 *p4 k3* to end
Rows 3-4: as 1-2
Row 5: p3 *c4b p3* to end
Row 6: as row 2
Repeat rows 1-6 twice more, inc each end of size 1 and dec each end of size 2 on the last row. **124(134) sts**
Change to 4mm (US 5) needles and graph. Continue until work measures 82cm (32 ins.) *** Note patt row.
Shape neck: patt 45(50) sts turn,
Dec neck edge on next 2 rows. Cast off. Place centre 34 sts on holder. Rejoin yarn to remaining sts at neck edge and patt to end. Work * to *.

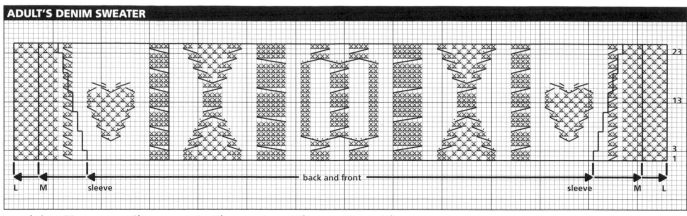

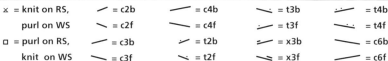

x	= knit on RS,	⟋	= c2b	⟋	= c4b	⟍	= t3b	⟍	= t4b
	purl on WS	⟍	= c2f	⟍	= c4f	⟍	= t3f	⟍	= t4f
▫	= purl on RS,	⟋	= c3b	⟋	= t2b	⟍	= x3b	⟍	= c6b
	knit on WS	⟍	= c3f	⟍	= t2f	⟍	= x3f	⟍	= c6f

FRONT

As back to 1 complete patt repeat (24 rows) less than *** noted patt row.
Shape neck: patt 55(60) sts turn,
on 55(60)sts: dec neck edge on next 6 rows. Dec neck edge on alt rows to 43(48) sts. Cont until work measures same as back at shoulder. Cast off.
Place centre 14 sts on holder.
Rejoin yarn to remaining sts at neck edge and patt to end. Work * to *.

SLEEVES

Using 3¼mm (US 3) needles cast on 52 sts and work 17 rows in cable rib as on back.
Row 18: rib 3 *inc, rib 4* 9 times, inc, rib 3.　　　　　　　　　　　　**62 sts**

Change to 4mm (US 5) needles and patt as follows:
Row 1: p16 k4 p5 k4 p4 k4 p5 k4 p16.
This sets patt as on centre back panel with 4 st cable and heart panel.
Cont in patt, inc each end of every 4th row to 104 sts, working extra sts into completion of 2 st twist, then p1, then moss stitch. Cont without shaping until work measures 56cm(22ins.). Cast off.

NECKBAND

Join right shoulder seam. With RS facing and using 3¼mm (US 3) needles pick up and knit 26 sts from side front neck, 14 sts from holder, 26 sts from side front neck, 3 sts from side back neck, 34 sts from

holder and 3 sts from side back neck.
Work as follows:
Row 1: k2 *p4 k3* 14 times, p4 k2
Row 2: p2 *k4 p3* 14 times, k4 p2
Row 3: as row 1
Row 4: p2 *c4b p3* 14 times, c4b p3
Rows 5-6 : as rows 1-2
Rows 7-11: as rows 1-5
Cast off loosely.

MAKING UP

Join left shoulder seam and neckband. Place sleeves into position and stitch. Join side and sleeve seams. Wash garment in hot wash and tumble dry.

STRIPY HAT

SIZES	1	2	3	4
to fit	1-3 yrs	4-6 yrs	7-10 yrs	adult

MATERIALS

Rowan Magpie Aran 100g hanks

M = natural 002	1	1	1	1
C = peony 306	1	1	1	1

1 pair each 3¾mm (US 4) and 4½mm (US 6) needles

TENSION

20 sts by 26 rows = 10cm (4ins) square over stocking stitch using 4½mm (US 6) needles.

ABBREVIATIONS

see page 80

METHOD

Using 3¾mm (US 4) needles and M cast on 81(91:99:109) sts and work 6(7:9:10)cm or 2½(3:3½:4)ins. in k1 p1 rib
Change to 4½mm (US 6) needles, moss

stitch and stripe patt:
Stripe patt = 4 rows contrast in moss stitch
　　　　　　4 rows main in moss stitch.
Continue in patt until work measures 20(22:24:26)cm or 8(9:9½:10)ins.
Shape Top, using C:
Row 1: k1(1:0:1) *k4 k2tog k4(4:5:6)* to end
Row 2: purl
Row 3: k1(1:0:1) *k3 k2tog k4(4:5:6)* to end
Row 4: purl
Row 5: k1(1:0:1) *k2 k2tog k4(4:5:6)* to end
Row 6: *p4(4:5:6) p2tog p1* to last

1(1:0:1) sts, pl(1:0:1)
Row 7: *k2tog* to last st, k1
Row 8: *p2tog* to end
Break yarn leaving long sewing thread.
Pass thread through remaining sts, pull tightly and secure. Stitch back seam.
Weave in any loose ends. Make pom-pom and attach to centre of top.

LADYBIRD SWEATER

Sizes	1	2	3	4	5
to fit years	1-2	3-4	5-6	7-8	9-10
actual chest cm(ins)	66(26)	69(27)	72(28½)	76(30)	80(31½)
back length cm(ins)	33(13)	38(15)	46(18)	50(19¾)	54(21)
sleeve seam cm(ins)	22(8½)	28(11)	31(12)	33(13)	36(14)

MATERIALS

Rowan Magpie Aran 100g balls

M = natural 002	4	5	5	6	7
A = peony 306	1	1	1	1	1
B = raven 062	1	1	1	1	1

1 pair each 3¾mm (US 4) and 4½mm (US 6) needles, stitch holders.

TENSION

20 sts by 26 rows = 10cm (4ins) square over stocking stitch using 4½mm (US 6) needles.

ABBREVIATIONS

see page 80

BACK

Using 3¾mm (US 4) needles and A cast on 64(68:72:76:80) sts. Change to M and work 8(8:10:10:10) rows in k2 p2 rib. Change to 4½mm (US 6) needles and stocking stitch. Continue until work measures18(20:24:32:35)cm or 7(8:9½: 12½:14)ins.

Shape armholes: cast off 3 (3.4:4:4) sts beg next 2 rows.

Continue until work measures 33(38:46: 50:54) cm or 13(15:18:19½:21)ins, ending with RS row.

Shape neck: WS facing, p19(20:21:22: 23), turn *dec neck edge on next 2 rows. Cast off.*

Place next 20(22:22:24:26) sts on holder. Rejoin yarn to remaining sts at neck edge and purl to end. Work * to *.

FRONT

Work rib as on back. Change to 4½mm (US 6) needles and stocking stitch. Work 8 (18:24:34:44) rows.

Place ladybird: k6(8:10:12:14) work row 1 of graph, k7(9:11:13:15).

Continue with graph as placed, shaping armholes as on back when work measures 18(20:24:32:37)cm or 7(8:9½:12½:14½)ins. Complete graph. Continue until work measures 28(33:40:45:50)cm or 11(13:16: 17½:19½)ins.

Shape neck: k24(26:26:28:30) turn, **dec neck edge on next 5(4:4:4:4) rows. Dec neck edge on alt rows to 17(18:19:20: 21) sts.

Continue without shaping until work measures same as back at shoulder. Cast off**.

Place next 10(10:12:12:12) sts on holder. Rejoin yarn to remaining sts at neck edge and knit to end. Work ** to **.

SLEEVES

Using 3¾mm (US 4) needles and A, cast on 32(32:36:36:40) sts. Change to M and work 8(8:10:10:10) rows in k2 p2 rib. Change to 4½mm (US 6) needles and stocking stitch. Inc each end of row 3 and every foll 5th row to 52(58:62:64:66) sts. Continue without shaping until work measures 22(28:30:33:35)cm or 8½ (11:12: 13:14)ins. Place markers at ends of last row. Work 4(4:5:5:5) more rows. Cast off.

NECKBAND

Join right shoulder seam. With RS facing and using 3¾mm (US 4) needles and M pick up and knit 14(14:16:16:16) sts from side front neck, 10(10:12:12:12) sts from holder, 14(14:16:16:16) sts from side front neck, 2 sts from side back neck, 20(22:22: 24:26) sts from holder and 2 sts from side back neck. Work 4(5:5:6:6) rows in k2 p2 rib. Cast off loosely using A.

MAKING UP

Join left shoulder seam and neckband. Join side seams. Set in sleevehead, markers to side seam, (see diagram on page 80). Stitch into position. Join sleeve seams. Weave in any loose ends.

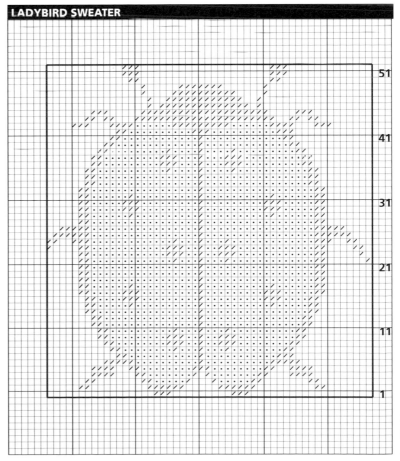

LADYBIRD SWEATER

☐ = natural
☒ = peony
☑ = raven

TARTAN JACKET

SIZES (CHILD)	1	2	3	4	5
to fit years	1-2	3-4	5-6	7-8	9-10
actual chest cm(ins)	71(28)	78(30½)	84(33)	89(35)	94(37)
back length cm(ins)	33(13)	38(15)	46(18)	51(20)	56(22)
sleeve seam cm(ins)	22(8½)	28(11)	31(12)	33(13)	36(14)

SIZES (ADULT)	6	7	8
to fit cm(ins)	89-94(35-37)	97-102(38-40)	104-109(41-43)
actual bust cm(ins)	104(41)	112(44)	120(47)
back length cm(ins)	68(27)	68(27)	68(27)
sleeve seam cm(ins)	46(18)	46(18)	46(18)

MATERIALS

Rowan Magpie Aran 100g hanks

SIZES	1	2	3	4	5	6	7	8
woodland 300	1	1	1	1	1	10	11	12
peony 306	4	4	5	6	7	2	2	2
speedwell 508	1	1	1	1	1	2	2	2
pumice 301	1	1	1	1	1	2	2	2

1 pair each 3¾mm (US 4) and 4½mm (US 6) needles, 5(5:5:5:5:6:6:6) buttons, stitch holders.

TENSION

20 sts by 26 rows = 10cm (4ins) square over stocking stitch using 4½mm (US 6) needles.

ABBREVIATIONS

see page 80

BACK

Using 3¾mm(US 4) needles and M cast on 64(68:72:76:80:94:100:106) sts and work 8(8:8:8:8:10:10:10) rows in moss stitch. Change to 4½mm (US 6) needles and stocking stitch. Cont until work measures 18(20:24:32:37:43:43:43)cm or 7(8:9¼:12¼:

14¼:17:17:17)ins.
Shape armholes: cast off 3(3:3:3:3:5:5:6) sts beg next 2 rows.
Work 36(40:44:46:48:66:66:66) rows from graph noting that patt is 36-row repeat.
Shape neck: patt 19(20:22:23:24:28:31: 33) sts, cast off 20(22:22:24:26:28:28:28) sts, patt to end.
Dec neck edge on next 2 rows. Cast off.
Rejoin yarns to remaining sts at neck edge and work * to *.

POCKETS (2)

Using 4½mm (US 6) needles and M cast on 20(20:20:20:20:24:24:24) sts and work 10(14:16:18: 22:30:30:30) rows in

stocking stitch. Leave on holder.

LEFT FRONT

Using 3¾mm (US 4) needles and M cast on 31(33:35:37:39:46:49:52) sts and work 8(8:8:8:8:10:10:10) rows in moss stitch. Change to 4½mm (US 6) needles and stocking stitch. Work 10(14:16:18:22:30: 30:30) rows. **Place pocket**. K6(7:8:9:10:11: 13:14) sts, place next 20 (20:20:20:20:24: 24:24) sts on holder, knit across pocket sts, k5(6:7:8:9:11:12:14). Cont until work measures 18(20:24:32:37: 43:43:43)cm or 7(8:9¼:12¼:14¼:17:17: 17)ins.
Shape armhole: Cast off 3(3:3:3:3:5:5:6) sts, work to end.

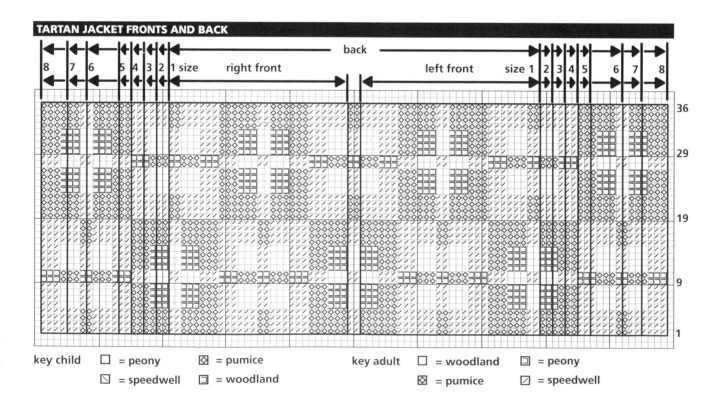

TARTAN JACKET FRONTS AND BACK

key child □ = peony ⊠ = pumice ◨ = speedwell ▦ = woodland

key adult □ = woodland ◩ = peony ⊠ = pumice ◨ = speedwell

Next row: purl
Work 24(28:30:32:34:50:50:50) rows from graph. *Work 1 more row*.
Shape neck: WS facing, cast off 4(4:5:5:6:6:6)sts, patt to end.
Dec neck edge on next 5(4:4:4:4:6:6:6) rows.
Dec neck edge on alt rows to 17(18:19:20:21:26:29:31) sts.
Work to match back length at shoulder. Cast off.

RIGHT FRONT
As left front reversing all shapings and omitting the *work 1 more row*.

SLEEVES
Using 3¾mm (US 4) needles and M cast on 31(33:35:37:39:49:49:49) sts and work 8(8:8:8:8:10:10:10) rows in moss stitch. Change to 4½mm (US 6) needles and stocking stitch. Inc. each end of 3rd and every following 5(5:5:5:4:4:4:4)th row to

51(59:61:63:65:91:91:91) sts. Cont without shaping until work measures 22(28:31:33:36:46:46:46)cm or 8½ (11:12:13:14:18:18:18)ins. Place markers at each end. Work a further 4(4:4:4:4:6:6:8) rows. Cast off.

BUTTONBAND
Using 3¾mm (US 4) needles and M, cast on 7(7:7:7:7:9:9:9) sts and work in moss stitch until band, when slightly stretched, fits front edge. Sew into place.

BUTTONHOLE BAND
As buttonband but make 5(5:5:5:5:6:6:6) buttonholes, evenly spaced along band, the first and last 1cm(½in)from top and bottom edges. Sew into place.
Make buttonhole:
Row 1: moss 3(3:3:3:3:4:4:4), cast off 1st, moss 3(3:3:3:3:4:4:4)
Row 2: moss 3(3:3:3:3:4:4:4), yrn, moss 3(3:3:3:3:4:4:4)

COLLAR
Join shoulder seams. Using 3¾mm (US 4) needles and M with RS facing, pick up and knit 67 (69:73:75:77:85:85:85) sts around neck, starting and finishing at centre of front bands and work as follows:
Rows 1-2: k2, moss to last 2sts, k2
Row 3: k2, moss to last 3sts, inc, k2
Repeat row 3 until work measures 6(6:6:6:6:8:8:8)cm or 2½(2½:2½:2½:2½:3¼:3¼:3¼)ins. Cast off.

POCKET TOP
Using 3¾mm (US 4) needles and M work 4(4:4:4:4:6:6:6) rows in moss stitch. Cast off.

MAKING UP
Join side seams. Set in sleeves, marker to side seams (see diagram on page 80). Join sleeve seams. Slipstitch pocket and pocket tops into place. Sew on buttons. Weave in any loose ends.

TIGER WAISTCOAT

Sizes child	1	2	3	4	5
to fit years	1-2	3-4	5-6	7-8	9-10
actual chest cm(ins)	56(22)	61(24)	66(26)	71(28)	76(30)
back length cm(ins)	31(12)	35(14)	40(16)	43(17)	46(18)

Sizes adult	S		M		L
to fit cm(ins)	82-87(32-34)		87-92(34-36)		92-97(36-38)
actual bust cm(ins)	92(36)		97(38)		102(40)
back length cm(ins)	51(20)		53(21)		56(22)

MATERIALS
Rowan Designer Double Knitting wool 50g balls

SIZES	1	2	3	4	5
M = orange 699	4	4	4	5	6
black 062	2	2	2	3	4
ADULT SIZES	S		M		L
M = orange 699	7		8		9
black 062	4		4		4

1 pair each 3mm (US 2) and 3¾mm (US 4) needles, 4(4:4:4:4:5:5:5) buttons

TENSIONS
24 sts by 32 rows = 10cm (4ins) square over stocking stitch using 3¾mm (US 4) needles.

ABBREVIATIONS
see page 80

BACK
Using 3mm (US 2) needles and M cast on 65(71:77:83:89:103:109:115) sts and work 10 rows in moss stitch.
Change to 3¾mm (US 4) needles and stocking stitch. Follow graph.

RIGHT AND LEFT FRONTS
Using 3mm (US 2) needles and M cast on

32(35:38:41:44:51:54:57) sts and work 10 rows in moss stitch.
Change to 3¾mm (US 4) needles and stocking stitch. Follow graph.

ARMBANDS
Join shoulder seams. Using 3mm (US 2) needles and M pick up and knit 73(77:85:89:95:139:145:149) sts around armhole. Work 5(5:5:5:5:7:7:7) rows in moss stitch. Cast off loosely in moss stitch.

BUTTONBAND
Using 3mm (US 2) needles and M cast on 6(6:6:6:6:9:9:9) sts and work in moss stitch. Make 4(4:4:4:4:5:5:5) buttonholes placing the first 1cm(½in) from cast on and

the last at start of V-shaping, and the other 2(2:2:2:2:3:3:3) evenly spaced between. To make buttonhole:
Row 1: moss 2(2:2:2:2:3:3:3) sts, cast off 2(2:2:2:2:3:3:3) sts, moss 2(2:2:2:2:3:3:3) sts
Row 2: moss 2(2:2:2:2:3:3:3) sts, cast on 2(2:2:2:2:3:3:3)sts, moss 2(2:2:2:2:3:3:3) sts.
Cont band until it fits around front edge. Cast off.

MAKING UP
Join side seams. Attach buttonband. Sew on buttons. Weave in any loose ends.

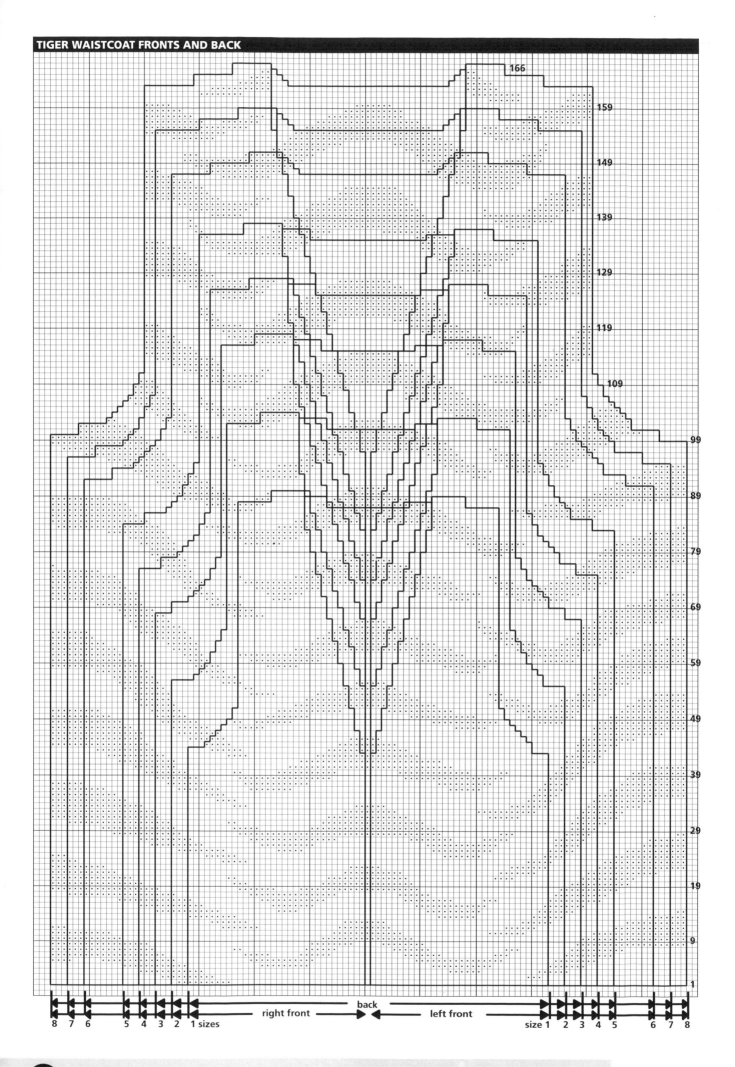

STRIPES AND SPOTS SWEATER

Sizes	1	2	3
to fit years	1-2	3-4	5-6
actual chest cm(ins)	69(27)	77(30)	85(33½)
back length cm(ins)	35(14)	41(16)	47(18½)
sleeve seam cm(ins)	22(8½)	28(11)	30(12)

MATERIALS

Rowan Handknit DK Cotton 50g balls

SIZES	1	2	3
M = turkish plum 277	5	6	7
A = rosso 215	1	1	1
B = sunkissed 231	1	1	1
C = lime 234	1	1	1
D = flame 254	1	1	1
E = basil 221	1	1	1

1 pair each 3¼mm (US 3) and 4mm (US 5) needles, stitch holders.

TENSION

20 sts by 28 rows = 10cm (4ins) square over stocking stitch using 4mm (US 5) needles.

ABBREVIATIONS

see page 80

BACK

Using 3¼mm (US 3) needles and M cast on 69(77:85) sts and work 10 rows in moss stitch.
Change to 4mm (US 5) needles, stocking stitch and stripe patt:
Stripe patt = 16 row repeat
Rows 1-8 : contrast
Rows 9-16: M
Work contrast stripes 1st A, 2nd B, 3rd C etc.
Work 48(60:82) rows in patt..
Shape armholes: cast off 4 sts beg next 2 rows.
Continue in stripe patt to completion of row 81(99:117).
Shape neck: WS facing: p19(22:25) turn *on 19(22:25) sts, dec neck edge on next 2 rows. Cast off.*
Place centre 23(25:27) sts on holder. Rejoin yarn to remaining sts at neck edge and purl to end. Work * to *.

FRONT

As back to completion of row 70(88:104).
Shape neck: RS facing: k24(28:32) sts, turn
*on 24(28:32) sts, dec neck edge on next 5 rows.
Row 6: knit
Row 7: dec neck edge, purl
Work rows 6-7 1(2:3) more times
17(20: 23) sts.
Continue to completion of row 84(102: 120). Cast off *
Place centre 13 sts on holder. Rejoin yarn to remaining sts at neck edge, knit to end. Work * to *.

SLEEVES

Using 3¾mm (US 4) needles and M cast on 35(37:39) sts and work 10 rows in moss stitch. Change to 4mm (US 5) needles and stocking stitch. Follow graph.

NECKBAND

Join right shoulder seam. With RS facing and using 3¼mm (US 3) needles and M pick up and knit 14(14:16) sts from side front neck, 13 sts from holder, 14(14:16)sts from side front neck, 3 sts from side back neck, 23(25:27) sts from holder and 3 sts from side back neck. Work 5 rows in moss stitch. Cast off loosely in moss stitch.

MAKING UP

Join left shoulder seam and neckband. Join side seams. Set in sleeve head, placing markers to side seam (see diagram on page 80). Stitch into place. Join sleeve seams. Weave in any loose ends.

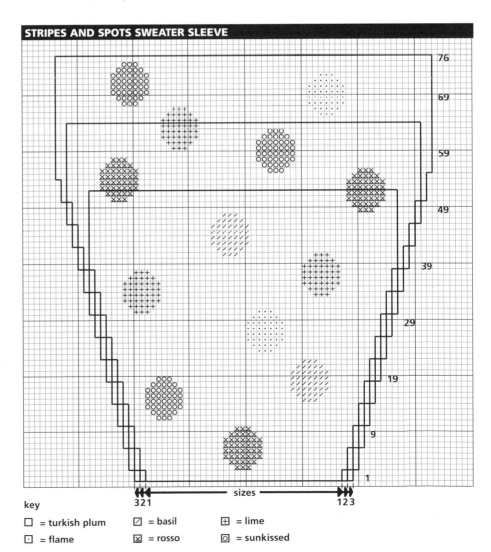

STRIPES AND SPOTS SWEATER SLEEVE

key

□ = turkish plum	☑ = basil	⊞ = lime
⊡ = flame	☒ = rosso	⊙ = sunkissed

PATTERN INFORMATION & SUPPLIERS

ABBREVIATIONS
The following abbreviations are those most commonly used in all the patterns. Where individual patterns have special abbreviations, these are explained at the beginning of the patterns. Where cast-off stitches are given in the middle of a row, the last stitch of the cast off is always included in the following instructions.

k	= knit
p	= purl
st(s)	= stitch(es)
RS	= right side
WS	= wrong side
inc	= increase by knitting into the front and back of next stitch
dec	= decrease by knitting the next 2 stitches together
tog	= together
beg	= beginning
patt	= pattern
alt	= alternate
foll	= following
cont	= continue
rem	= remaining
cn	= cable needle
yrn	= yarn around needle
sl	= slip next stitch
psso	= pass slipped stitch over
k2 tog	= knit next 2 stitches together
p2 tog	= purl next 2 stitches together
M	= main colour
C	= contrast colour
* *	= repeat enclosed instructions number of times indicated by numeral
( )	= brackets refer to larger size(s). Where only one figure is given this refers to all sizes
[ ]	= repeat enclosed instructions as indicated by numeral

stocking stitch = row 1: knit, row 2: purl

moss stitch = (on even number of sts)
 row 1: *k1 p1* to end
 row 2: *p1 k1* to end
 = (on odd number of sts)
 every row: *k1 p1* to last st, k1.

k1 p1 rib = (on even number of sts)
 every row: *k1 p1* to end.
 = (on odd number of sts)
 row 1: *k1 p1* to last st, k1
 row 2: k1 *k1 p1* to end

GLOSSARY OF TERMS
Tension	=	gauge
cast off	=	bind off
moss stitch	=	seed stitch
stocking stitch	=	stockinette stitch
colour	=	shade

If you wish the charts may be enlarged on a photocopier.

Zoë Mellor can be contacted at:
Ground Floor, 26 Belvedere Terrace, Brighton, East Sussex, England BN1 3AF.

HOW TO DO A TENSION SQUARE
Cast on at least 30 sts and work at least 40 rows. Measure only the sts given (eg 22 sts by 28 rows) to check the needle size. Remember that one st too many or too few over 10cm or 4ins can spoil your work. If you have too many stitches, change to a larger sized needle, or if you have too few, change to a smaller size, and try again until the tension square is correct.
Note: yarns from different manufacturers may not knit to these tensions.

IMPORTANT NOTE ON COLOUR KNITTING
In the patterns you are advised to use "block knitting" or "intarsia" technique. This means using separate balls of contrast colours, or shorter lengths wound around bobbins, but NOT carrying the main yarn across the back of the section. This is partly to avoid bulky knitting, but mainly to avoid pulling in the work which reduces the size of the motifs and distorts the knitting, even changing the size of the garment. Please work these areas with separate yarns, twisting them at the colour change to avoid holes forming.

CARE INSTRUCTIONS
Steam the knitting lightly using a warm iron over a damp cloth. Never let the iron come directly into contact with the knitting. Ease the knitting into shape, or block it out with pins until the steam has completely dried off. If the tension is correct, and yet the completed garment is slightly smaller than it should be, do not worry. Often, especially with textured stitches – particularly cables – the knitting is more springy when brand new and will relax to size when worn or washed. For washing instructions, see ball bands.

ACKNOWLEDGMENTS
Thank you to all the fabulous knitters who knitted up my designs with such care and attention, especially Eva, Gill, Maxine, Mandy and Linda. Special thanks to Eva who knitted, pattern checked and assisted me with every aspect of this book and who has encouraged and supported me in realising my ideas as a knitwear designer. Thank you also to all the models who look great in my designs! Thank you to Joey Toller for the beautiful photographs. Thank you to everyone at Godstone Farm, Kent for their help and hospitality. Thanks also to Cindy and Kate at Collins & Brown for their guidance and enthusiasm. Last, but by no means least, thank you to my parents and to Tim for their help and support.

SUPPLIERS OF ROWAN YARNS
Australia MacEwen Enterprises, 1/178 Cherry Lane, Laverton North, Vic 3026. Tel: 03 9369 3998
Belgium Hedera, Pleinstraat 68, 3001 Leuven. Tel: 016 232189.
Canada Diamond Yarns, 9697 St Laurent, Montreal, Que H3L 2N1. Tel: 514 388 6188.
Denmark Filcolana A/S, Hagemannsvej 26-28, Box 151, 8600 Silkeborg. Tel: 86 81 02 11.
France Elle Tricote, 52 Rue Principale, 67300 Schiltigheim. Tel: 388 62 65 31.
Germany Wolle & Design, Wolfshovener Strasse 76, 52428 Julich-Stetternich. Tel: 02461 54735.
Holland Henk & Henrietta Beukers, Dorpsstraat 9, NL-5327 AR Hurwenen. Tel: 0418 661764.
Italy La Compagnia Del Cotone, Via Mazzini 44, 1-10123 Torino. Tel: 011 87 83 81.
New Zealand MacEwen Enterprises Ltd, 24b Allright Place, Mt Wellington, Auckland. Tel: 09527 3241.
Norway Eureka, PO Box 357, N1401 Ski. Tel: 64 86 55 40.
Sweden Wincent Sveavagen 94, 11350 Stockholm. Tel 08 673 70 60.
UK Rowan Yarns, Green Mill Lane, Holmfirth, West Yorkshire, HD7 1RW. Tel: 01484 681881.
USA Westminster Fibres Inc, 5 Northern Boulevard, Amherst, New Hampshire 03031. Tel: 063 886 5041/5043.

HOW TO FIT SQUARE SLEEVE
Sleeve must fit in squarely
fit **A** to **A**
B to **B**
C to **C**

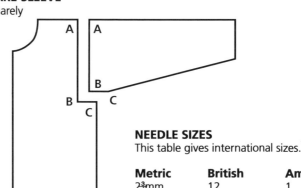

NEEDLE SIZES
This table gives international sizes.

Metric	British	American
2¾mm	12	1
3mm	11	2
3¼mm	10	3
3¾mm	9	4
4mm	8	5
4½mm	7	6

The Man Made of Stars

Written by M.H. Clark · Illustrated by Lisa Evans

One night, as I lay in bed, I looked out the window at the huge, round moon and the dark night sky, and I saw something...

A little light flickering, far away. I watched as it moved along the edge of the trees until I couldn't see it anymore. I tried to fall asleep, but I lay awake and wondered. It seemed like such a mystery.

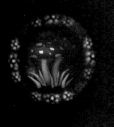

I asked my grandmother.

"Oh, yes," she said, "that must be the man made of stars. Every evening, when the sky is painted pink and blue and gold, the man made of stars sets off to work. He walks along the path where the forest meets the field, with a bag on his back and a lantern in his hands. If you see him as he goes along his way, you will see a twinkle at the edge of the trees like a comet or a firefly."

"Is he magic?" I asked.

"No one knows," she said, "but he has
lived here always."

"But what does he do?" I asked. "Why do they call him the man made of stars?"

"No one remembers that anymore," my grandmother said. She smiled and she sipped her tea.

Sometimes, I thought I saw the man
made of stars in town. His eyes shined
like there was a great secret he knew.

I wished I knew his secret, too.
It seemed to make him so happy.

"Next time, I will ask him,"
I always thought. But next
time I was always too shy.

One summer night, I couldn't sleep. The windows were open wide, and a warm breeze lifted my curtains like they were sails. I looked outside to where the grasses blew and rippled like waves on the sea.

Suddenly, a light sparkled in the distance.

I crept down the stairs and out the door, silent
as a cat. I crossed the field where the grasses
stood tall and dry in the light of the moon.
The ground was warm under my feet.

"Wait!" I called out, but the flickering
light moved on.

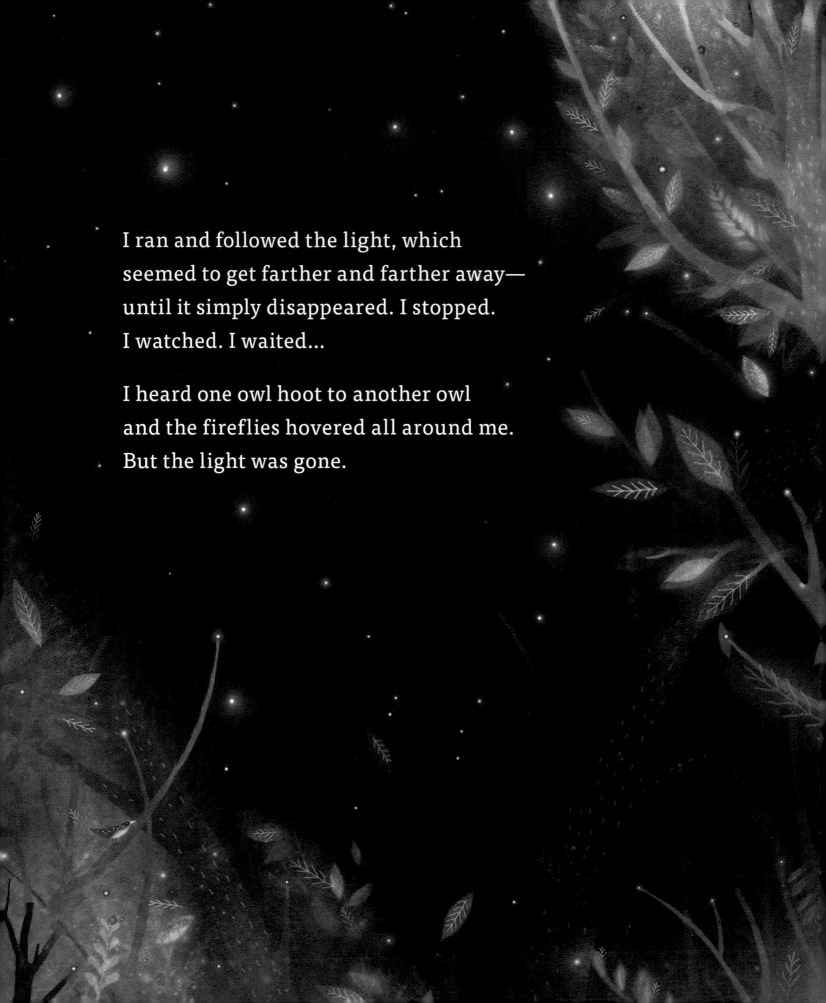

I ran and followed the light, which
seemed to get farther and farther away—
until it simply disappeared. I stopped.
I watched. I waited...

I heard one owl hoot to another owl
and the fireflies hovered all around me.
But the light was gone.

Just then, the light
began to climb the hill!
So I climbed, too.

At the top of the hill, I saw the strangest, most wonderful sight. The man made of stars reached into his bag and pulled out a beautiful glowing thing—something that seemed to be made entirely out of light.

He held it and then threw it, and the glittering light floated higher and higher until it became another star in the sky.

The man made of stars reached into his bag again and pulled out another glowing light. It was so beautiful that I walked up to see it closely.

"What is it?" I asked.

"Well," he said, "this one must be pure love. See how bright it is?"

"Where do you find them?"

"Oh, they're everywhere," he said. "Look up at the stars. What do you see?"

"They glow."

"And so do you," he said. "You are made of kindness and possibility and brilliance. Everything you are made of, the stars are made of. And though the stars shine only at night, when it is dark, your light shines always."

"Why do they call you man who is made of stars?" I asked.

He laughed and then said, "Is that what they call me? Well, you are made of stars, too. We all are."

He reached into his bag again. "Here," he said, "this one is yours." And he placed the warm, glowing light in my hand.

"You must have made someone very happy today. When you shared that kindness, a little extra spilled over. Now that kindess will become a new star."

I held my star up and let it go.

Now, each day when the sun sets and night begins—when the sky is painted pink and blue and gold—I look up to see if there is a new star in the sky.

Maybe one I will recognize because it's made from a special piece of me.

The end.

COMPENDIUM.
live inspired

WITH SPECIAL THANKS TO THE ENTIRE COMPENDIUM FAMILY.

CREDITS:
Written by: M.H. Clark
Illustrated by: Lisa Evans
Edited by: Amelia Riedler
Creative Direction by: Julie Flahiff

Library of Congress Control Number: 2014959335
ISBN: 978-1-938298-61-5

1st printing. Printed in China with soy inks. A051503001